$1.8(C°) + 32 = F°$

VISITORS' GUIDE TO ZIMBABWE

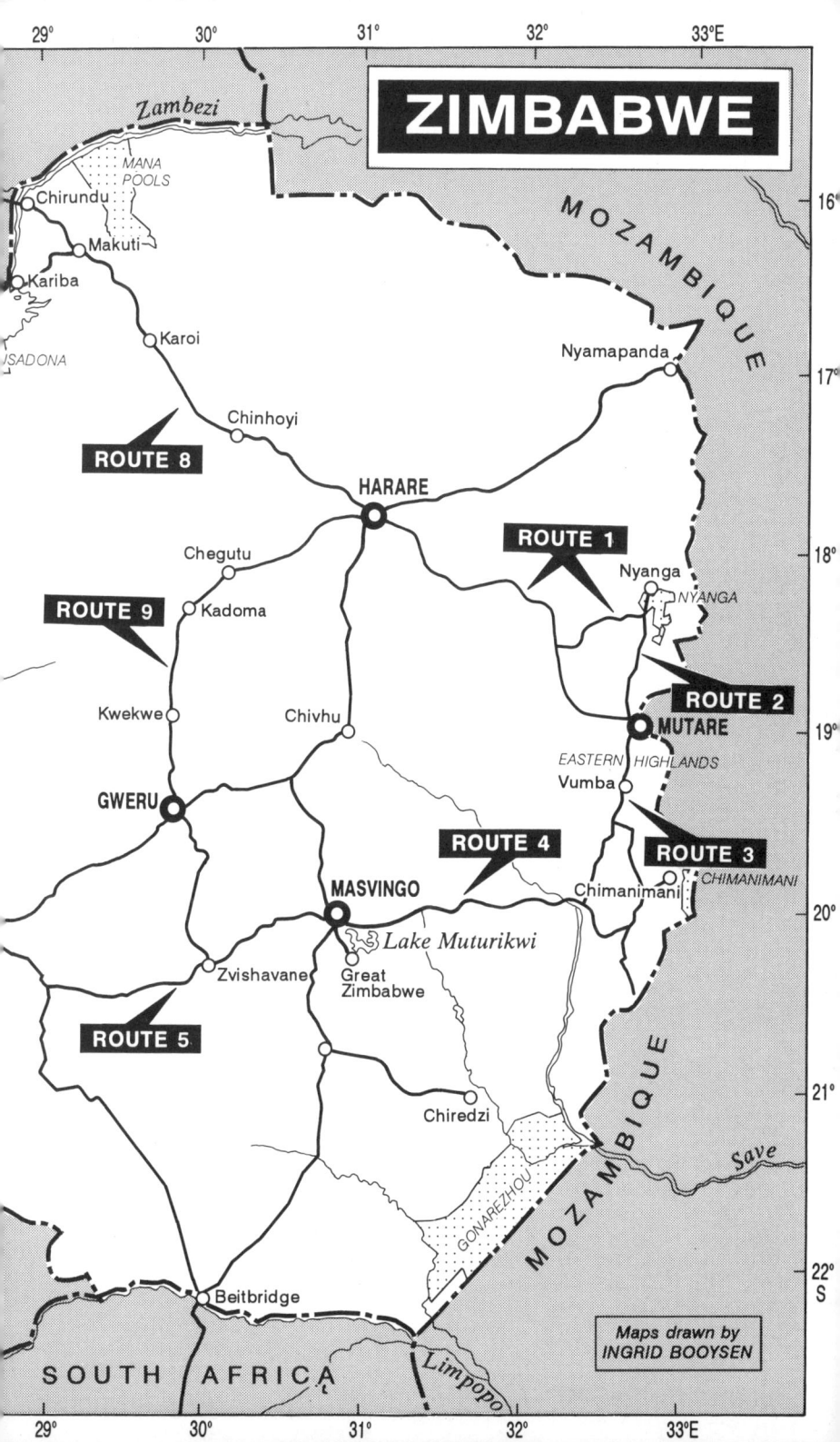

VISITORS' GUIDE TO ZIMBABWE

HOW TO GET THERE · WHAT TO SEE · WHERE TO STAY

Martine Maurel

SOUTHERN
BOOK PUBLISHERS

Visitors' Guide to Zimbabwe
Copyright © 1993 by Martine Maurel

All rights reserved. No part of this publication may be reproduced or transmitted in any form or by any means without prior written permission from the publisher.

ISBN 1 86812 425 8

First edition, first impression 1993

Published by
Southern Book Publishers (Pty) Ltd
PO Box 3103, Halfway House, 1685, South Africa

While the author and publisher have endeavoured to verify all facts, they will not be held responsible for any inconvenience that may result from possible inaccuracies in this book.

Published in the USA by
Hunter Publishing Inc
300 Ratitan Centre Parkway
Edison NJ 08818
(908) 225 1900 Fax (908) 4170842

Published in the UK by
Mooreland Publishing Co Ltd
Moor Farm Road West
Airfield Estate
Ashbourne
Derbyshire
DE6 1HD

ISBN 0 86190 276 9

Cover photograph by Anthony Bannister Photographic Library
Cover design by Insight Graphics
Set on 10 on 11.5 pt Palatino
by Kohler Carton & Print (Natal)
Printed and bound by Kohler Carton & Print (Natal)

AUTHOR'S NOTE

Since Zimbabwe's independence many names of places and streets have changed. If you are familiar with the old names please consult page 107 for a list of name changes.

Since this book was written Zimbabwe, along with other countries in the region, has suffered its worst drought in living memory. This may cause conditions to vary from those described in the book.

Acknowledgement

The author wishes to express her appreciation to Antony Phillips and Michael Harrold for their assistance in reading over the text and making constructive comments.

CONTENTS

How to use this guide 1

1. THE FACTORS THAT SHAPE ZIMBABWE 3
Geography and climate 3
Vegetation 4
Economy 4
History 5
Population 7
Government 8

2. WHERE TO GO 9
Harare 9
Bulawayo 18
National Parks 24
Great Zimbabwe 47
Lake Kariba and its shoreline 49
Victoria Falls 57

3. WHAT TO DO 62
Walking and hiking 62
Watersport 66
Birdwatching 68
Craft and souvenir hunting 70
Angling 75
For safari enthusiasts 76
Other sports 89

4. HOW TO GET THERE 93
By air 93
By road 94
Getting into Zimbabwe 96

5. TRAVELLING INSIDE ZIMBABWE 101

Road transport 101
Standard routes 112
Air transport 123
Rail transport 124
Boat transport 125

6. FACTORS AFFECTING HOLIDAY PLANNING 126

Seasons and climate 126
Health precautions 128
Safety precautions 133
What to take 133

7. WHERE TO STAY 136

Accommodation listed by town/resort 136
National Parks accommodation 155
Restaurants in the main centres 160

8. MISCELLANEOUS INFORMATION 165

Index 181

HOW TO USE THIS GUIDE

Chapter 1 offers some background on Zimbabwe's history and the forces that have shaped the country.

Armed with this broad perspective, consult Chapter 2 to decide which places you would like to visit, taking into account your possible special interests, outlined in Chapter 3.

Once you have decided which destinations you wish to visit, read Chapter 4, which explains how to get to Zimbabwe by road, train or air, and what formalities and practical considerations will apply once you enter the country.

Chapter 5 explains the different methods of travel available in Zimbabwe and also provides a description of the standard routes you might take to get from place to place.

Chapter 6 provides information on certain factors that may affect the timing of your visit, how to avoid illness and what to do if it does strike; safety precautions and what you might consider bringing with you into the country to make your stay more pleasurable. Having decided which areas you wish to visit, how to get there and what you would like to do during your stay, consult Chapter 7 to plan your accommodation.

Finally, Chapter 8 contains miscellaneous information that may come in handy when you plan your trip or while you are in Zimbabwe.

1. THE FACTORS THAT SHAPE ZIMBABWE

"Zimbabwe" means "house of stone" in the indigenous Shona language – a name first given to the Great Zimbabwe ruins in the south of the country which housed its first ancient civilisation.

GEOGRAPHY AND CLIMATE

Situated between 15° and 22° south of the equator and between 25° and 30° east, the country forms part of tropical southern Africa. Landlocked Zimbabwe borders on Botswana to the west, Zambia to the north, Mozambique to the east and South Africa to the south.

Shaped like a teapot, Zimbabwe lies between the natural borders formed in the north by the Zambezi, the fourth largest river in Africa, and to the south and west by the Limpopo River. The Eastern Highlands create another border in the east.

About three times the size of England and almost the size of California, Zimbabwe covers an area of over 390 000 km², of which an important feature is the extensive Lake Kariba. Created in the late 1950s, Kariba is the third largest manmade dam in Africa after the Aswan Dam in Egypt and Cahora Bassa in neighbouring Mozambique. There are no natural lakes in Zimbabwe but more than 7 000 dams have been built to store water as rainfall during the short rainy season mainly consists of heavy, brief storms with rapid water run-off.

Almost the entire county lies over 300 m above sea level. A major feature that influenced settlement and agriculture was the central plateau or "highveld" running from the north-east to the south-west. Forming the country's backbone, the plateau is 650 km long and 80 km wide and over 1 200 m above sea level. It lies atop the famous Great Dyke, with its rich deposits of gold, gemstones and minerals, and contains the highest concentration of commercial farms in Zimbabwe.

The so-called "highveld" is flanked by the "middleveld", which ranges between 600 m and 1 200 m above sea level. In turn the middleveld is bordered by the hot "lowveld", only 300 m to 600 m above sea level. Zimbabwe's 350 km-long mountainous region to the east, known as the Eastern Highlands, reaches its highest point at Mount Nyangani (2 593 m). Zimbabwe's lowest point is just 162 m above sea level and is at the junction of the Save and Runde rivers at the extreme southeast on the border with Mozambique.

Although it lies within the tropics, Zimbabwe does not conform to the stereotype of the typically tropical country. This is because varied altitudes influence its markedly temperate climate, which has two main seasons: the hot/wet and the dry/cool. (See more on climate in Chapter 6 – Factors affecting holiday planning, page 126.)

Temperatures range from freezing at the highest altitudes in the winter months to above 40 °C at the lowest altitude in the summer months. The wet season is short, generally lasting from November to March.

VEGETATION

The country can be divided into five major regions:

- Victoria Falls and Hwange in the east
- The lowveld in the south
- Kariba and the Zambezi Valley to the north
- The Eastern Highlands
- The central plateau

Within these regions you'll see vegetation ranging from arid scrub and the grey-green fuzz of thorn trees to never-ending vistas of golden savanna and pine plantations. The indigenous msasa tree, whose new spring leaves are illogically orange and blood-red and change slowly to bright green in summer, will create a lasting impression.

ECONOMY

Zimbabwe's largest foreign exchange earners are the agricultural and mining sectors. The most important crop is tobacco followed by maize, cotton, coffee and tea. Zimbabwe is the world's third largest exporter of flue-cured leaf tobacco. Minerals mined include coal, gold, chrome, asbestos and copper.

HISTORY

Prehistory–A.D. 1100

Early settlement by nomadic Bushmen (San) is indicated by extensive archeological evidence, including the world's most concentrated collection of rock art or cave paintings.

Coming from the north, Bantu migrants settled in Zimbabwe on their journey south and by A.D. 800 groups such as the Tonga and the Tavara were identifiable. These occupied the northerly Zambezi Valley area while the Karanga settled where present-day Masvingo Province lies in the southern part of Zimbabwe.

1250–1450

The large citadel of Great Zimbabwe was built in what is now Masvingo Province to house the Karanga king during relatively prosperous times while gold was being mined and exported and trade routes opened with China and Arabia. Other similar, but smaller, citadels were built elsewhere in Zimbabwe, the most notable of which can be found at Khame (also spelt Khami) near Bulawayo.

1450–1600

The Torwa dynasty took over from the Karanga and based their kingdom at Khame. Their buildings showed the same degree of sophistication as those of the Karanga but were smaller in scale. As it was dependent on gold exports for its prosperity, the Torwa's economy began crumbling when exports slowed and finally collapsed at the end of the seventeenth century.

1450–1700

At the same time the Mutapa state was developing wider control to the north while interacting with Portuguese explorers, who had made attempts to colonise parts of Zimbabwe. They had heard stories about the gold reserves to be found there from the Arab traders who were the first outsiders to explore the region.

By the eighteenth century, the Mutapa state had declined in power, largely as a result of its association with the Portuguese who effectively controlled the state.

1680–1840

The Rozvi empire emerged from the remnants of the old Torwa state that had settled in Danangombe (to the north of Bulawayo) after moving there from Khame. Led by the militant Changamire, the Rozvi were an offshoot of the Mutapa state and wielded power as far east as Manicaland. Much of their wealth was based on military power and their ability to exact tribute from fearful peasants. Unwilling to be dominated by the Portuguese as their Mutapa predecessors had been, they drove the Portuguese out of Zimbabwe. The power of the Rozvi began to decline in the nineteenth century.

1800–1890

Ndebele, also known as Matabele, fleeing from tribal wars in South Africa, crossed the Limpopo and settled in the west of the present-day Zimbabwe. Led by Mzilikazi, they formed a capital at Bulawayo in the 1840s and eventually came to dominate a number of smaller groups including some Shona.

On Mzilikazi's death in 1870, his son Lobengula took over leadership of the clan. They subsequently controlled the area until Cecil Rhodes' invading forces brought about their downfall in 1893.

1890–1980

The discovery of rich gold deposits in South Africa resulted in prospectors turning their gaze north, where they thought even richer reserves might be found. Backed by the British Government, the wealthy Cecil John Rhodes, whose fortune had been amassed on the South African diamond fields, formed the British South Africa Company (BSAC). To cut a long story short, Rhodes and his company took over the territory by promising existing rulers wealth and goods which never materialised.

In 1896 the first Chimurenga or War of Liberation was waged by the Ndebele and Shona against the invading Europeans. It lasted six weeks before being suppressed. From that time until 1980, a white elite that in technical terms was overseen by Britain, ruled the black majority. With its borders already established, Zimbabwe, then known as Rhodesia (named after Cecil Rhodes), experienced its greatest growth both in terms of physical infrastructure and population.

Towards the latter part of this period, 1954–63, the colonial administration formed a Federation of Northern Rhodesia (Zambia), Nyasaland (Malawi) and Southern Rhodesia (present-day Zimbabwe), but the idea was ill-fated and wracked with nationalist opposition that led to the breakdown of the Federation and to independence being granted to Zambia and Malawi.

The second Chimurenga war began in 1966, a year after the Unilateral Declaration of Independence (UDI) declared by Ian Smith, then prime minister of the white government. The new Zimbabwean state was ushered in in 1980 after a crippling thirteen-year civil war.

1980–present

In its first ten years in power, the new government, under Robert Mugabe, had to contend with drought, recession and initially, guerrilla activity. It has successfully overcome these hardships and the country is now at peace.

The ruling party is the ZANU (Zimbabwe African National Union)/Patriotic Front alliance which governs the country on the basis of an effective one-party system, although a one-party state has not been officially declared. The original intention by the new government to introduce marxist socialism to the country has been officially abandoned.

POPULATION

According to a 1991 estimate, the population numbers about ten million and grows annually by 3,5 per cent. Population density is about 65 people per square kilometre.

The two major ethnic groups are the Shona in the centre, north and east and the Ndebele in the western and southern parts of Zimbabwe.

Smaller indigenous groups include the Tonga, the Hlengwe and the Vendao. There are also small European (150 000), coloured or mixed race (30 000) and Asian (15 000) groups. English is the official language while Shona and Sindebele are the most widely spoken indigenous languages.

Harare's population is estimated at 900 000 while its dormitory city of Chitungwiza has a population of close to a million. Bulawayo has about 550 000 inhabitants and the next largest towns are Gweru in the centre and Mutare in the east of the country.

Zimbabwe is subdivided into the following administrative regions: Manicaland; Manicaland east; Mashonaland central, north, east and west; Matabeleland north and south; Midlands province and Masvingo province.

GOVERNMENT

Zimbabwe is an independent republic with an executive president. The government is based on a multi-party system, although the ruling party has such strong sway that the country seems to be a de facto one-party state. Elections are held every five years. Parliament is made up of a single chamber, currently headed by President Robert Mugabe.

The flag

The colours of the flag are green (for land), gold (for mineral wealth), red (for the blood that was shed in the cause of freedom) and black (for the country's people). There is a white triangle on the left of the flag which represents peace, with the Zimbabwe bird (of indeterminate species) behind which lies a red star, representing Zimbabwe's national hopes.

2. WHERE TO GO

Zimbabwe's vastness encompasses diverse tourist attractions, the more interesting of which are the main centres of Harare, Bulawayo, Mutare and Gweru; the national and recreational parks; Victoria Falls; Lake Kariba; Great Zimbabwe and the Eastern Highlands.

This section contains brief descriptions of each destination and offers suggestions of places to visit. Once you have decided whether you wish to visit a particular place, consult Chapter 7 – Where to stay (page 136) for information about accommodation.

HARARE

Before independence Zimbabwe's largest city and capital, Harare, was called Salisbury. The wheel of history has turned full circle in that it has been renamed after Chief Harare, who was headquartered here before the arrival of the British in 1890.

At first the new settlers held out hopes that it would be the centre of the second most important gold mining area after South Africa, and European inhabitants were enticed there with the promise of mining claims and land.

As Fort Salisbury, this marshy area was originally extremely isolated, but once the railway was built linking it to the outside world, development occurred at a much faster pace.

By 1935, light industries were springing up and the capital was firmly established as the industrial heart of what was then known as Southern Rhodesia.

At 1 500 m above sea level and with an annual rainfall of 760 mm, falling mainly between November and March, the climate offered a comfortable mildness without the risk of the tropical malaria found in the lower-lying areas.

Its wide tree-lined avenues set out in a regular grid pattern make Harare (meaning "the one who doesn't sleep") a pleasant and predictable city to explore on foot. Much remains to bear witness to its colonial past. Despite this the building hiatus that characterised the years between the 1960s and 1980s – when Rhodesia was lost in the

10 Zimbabwe

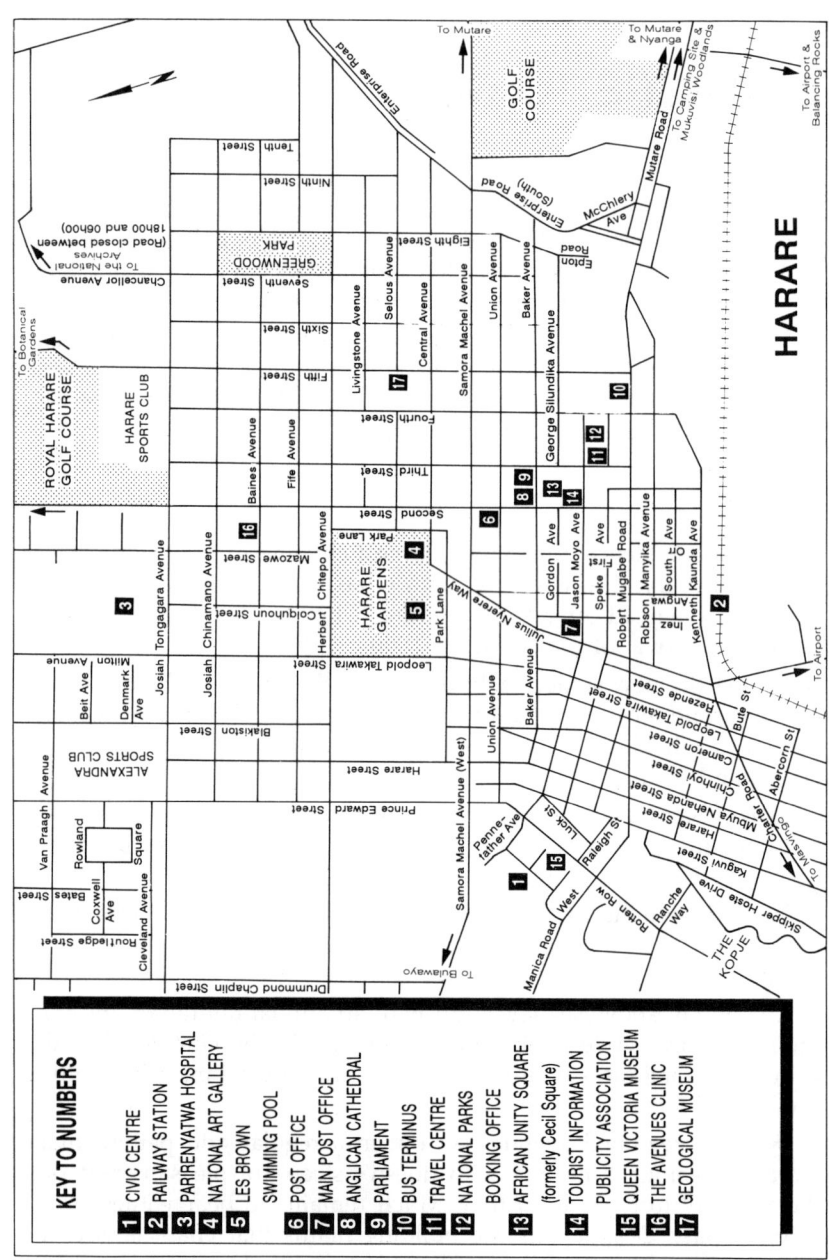

international political wilderness – is evident in the contrast between the grey, uninspired concrete architecture of the 1960s and the rare but more jazzy, glassfronted tower blocks of the '80s. Overall, Harare exudes a respectable and unspectacular conservatism.

A few buildings that were built much earlier this century can be spied dotted here and there as you explore the city. These include Cecil House, on the corner of Second Street and Central Avenue, which was constructed in 1901. Another is the old Lonrho building built in 1910 and situated on the corner of Baker Avenue and Third Street. The parliament buildings on the corner of Baker Avenue and Third Street, opposite the old Lonrho building, are almost a century old.

The main commercial sector is centred on African Unity Square (formerly Cecil Square), a small green oasis forming the heart of the city. First Street Mall, the city's main shopping area, lies one block to the west of African Unity Square. Even though foreign exchange controls have restricted the importation of foreign goods, the shop windows are packed with good quality locally made goods that bear testimony to the resourcefulness of this self-sufficient nation.

Zimbabwe's colonial past is evident in Harare's split personality. The sanitised, orderly commercial sector and what used to be the residential suburbs of white Harare contrast with the high-density, colourful bustle of Kopje (the black commercial sector before independence).

For those who want to see the other side of Harare a visit to Mbare (just 3 km from the centre) will be enlightening. The city's split personality is further evident in the mixture of nostalgic and unmistakeably British names such as Willoughby Crescent, Prince Edward Avenue and Rotten Row, and the newly emerging and proudly nationalistic African names, which largely commemorate the heroes of the struggle for independence.

Since independence, moves have been made countrywide to "Zimbabweanise" many place names as well as street names, a practice which may cause some confusion among tourists who have maps that are not completely up to date (see pages 107–10 for a list of streets and places which have had their names changed).

Despite its strong links with the relatively recent past when most of its development took place, Harare has kept pace with the times and offers the visitor many modern delights. Entertainment in the form of theatre, nightclubs, restaurants and cinemas is available, while shops strive to cater for most tastes.

The tourist with a couple of days to spend in the city will have ample time to search out and investigate just what interests him, whether it be rooted in African culture or the pseudo-European lifestyle.

If you are lucky enough to be there during October and November you will be dazzled by the unforgettable sight of the jacarandas in bloom. These magnificent flowering trees were originally imported from South America. As if to try and upstage the jacarandas the aptly named flamboyant bursts into bloom with its equally startling hues of vermilion in November and December.

Like the hub of a wheel, Harare is conveniently placed as a centre for visits to destinations north and west, south and east. Kariba in the north and Bulawayo in the south are just three and a half to four hours' drive from Harare, while the Eastern Highlands, Nyanga and Great Zimbabwe are just three hours to the east and south respectively.

Tourist information

Of interest to the tourist is the stretch of Jason Moyo Avenue between Second and Fourth Streets, which contains the information offices of the Publicity Association, travel agents, the air terminal from where the buses depart for the airport on the hour every hour, and the Zimbabwe Tourist Development Corporation, next door to the booking offices for National Parks and Zimbabwe Sun central reservations office. Try also the Harare Publicity Association on the corner of Second Street. If you wish to participate in a guided tour of the city, ask your hotel or the Publicity Association to recommend a tour operator.

Access

By air

The capital is served by Zimbabwe's international airport, Harare Airport, situated some 18 km from the city. An Air Zimbabwe bus leaves for the city on the hour every hour, stopping at the terminus in central Harare. No destination in Zimbabwe is more than an hour away by plane.

By train

The station is five streets to the south of African Unity Square, on Kenneth Kaunda Avenue.

By car

Harare is 352 km from Chirundu on the Zambian border, 245 km fom Nyamapanda on the Mozambique border, 579 km from Beitbridge on the South African border and 537 km from Plumtree on the Botswana border.

Accommodation and restaurants

See Chapter 7. Note that the top of the range hotels expect payment in foreign currency or require that you produce a bank receipt to show that you have exchanged currency to the value of your hotel bill. This applies mainly to foreigners coming from Europe, Asia, America and Australia whereas regional visitors coming from Zambia, Malawi, South Africa, Botswana, Lesotho, Swaziland and Namibia are often permitted to pay the same rate as Zimbabweans. However the situation seems very fluid and varies according to the establishment you stay in.

Places of interest in Harare

There are a number of tourist organisations that cater for visitors to Harare by taking them on special interest tours of the city. Your hotel will be able to put you in touch with these companies.

National archives

Borrowdale Road/Churchill Avenue. Open weekdays 07:45–16:30; Saturday 08:00 till noon. Closed on Sundays and public holidays. Considered to be the storehouse of the nation's history, the archives will appeal to history buffs with its collection of documents, books, sketches, diaries and maps as well as Thomas Baines paintings. Don't forget to take in the fascinating newspaper display and stamp collection. The archives also have reading rooms and a gallery.

Mbare market

From town find Cameron Street and continue south into Remembrance Drive. Turn left into Chamunika Street and continue for a short distance. The market is on your left. Open from 06:00 to 18:00. Known as the Mbare *musika*, this is the country's biggest traditional marketplace, attracting rural Zimbabweans like bees to a honey pot. Here you will find fresh and dried produce, secondhand clothes, chickens for the pot, traditional medicines and herbalists selling a wide variety of strange "medicines", including potions guaranteed to attract lovers, or even help your child succeed at school. It is an ideal sojourn for those who like to browse at length, and useful if you want to buy some souvenirs. Remember to be on the lookout for pickpockets.

National gallery

Corner of Julius Nyerere Way and Park Lane, just round the corner from the Monomotapa Hotel and adjacent to Harare gardens. Open Tuesday to Sunday 09:00 to 12:30 and 14:00 to 17:00. Regular exhibitions of indigenous and foreign art collections are held here. Large and modern, the gallery busily encourages an interest in the arts among the local community by putting on workshops, demonstrations, permanent and temporary exhibitions, films and talks. Shona sculpture, which enjoys a well deserved international reputation, is well represented and supported. Visit the permanent indoor collection and sculpture garden.

The superb permanent art collection upstairs features art from other parts of Africa and is certainly worth visiting. The gallery shop houses a large selection of local arts and crafts, including some captivating pieces of stone sculpture, hand-dyed fabrics, woollen rugs, baskets and pottery.

Watch out for the annual Zimbabwe Heritage Exhibition, which is usually staged from October till the end of the year.

National museum

Willoughby Crescent, off Jason Moyo Road (West) opposite the Civic Centre (open daily from 09:00 to 17:00). Depicts the history of man and animal in Mashonaland (the province in which Harare lies) in lifelike displays.

Harare gardens

Bounded by Leopold Takawira Street, Herbert Chitepo Avenue and Park Lane and overlooked by the Monomotapa Hotel. Harare's main park covers several hectares and includes a recreation area, open-air theatre and restaurant, bandstand, children's playground, bowling greens, cenotaph memorials to the dead of two world wars and a miniature model of Victoria Falls. Adjacent to the park is the Olympic-sized Les Brown swimming pool, a refreshing stopover if you have your trunks with you and feel like cooling off during "suicide month" – October. If you are there in December and have children with you, visit the section of the gardens near the Monomotapa Hotel where a fascinating collection of nursery rhyme characters can be viewed as part of Harare's Christmas lights display. It is recommended that you do not visit the Gardens at night.

Greenwood Park

Between Seventh and Eighth streets and Josiah Chinamano and Herbert Chitepo avenues. Open Saturday 14:00 to 17:30; Sunday 10:00 to 13:00 and 14:00 to 17:00.

When your children have had enough of sightseeing and shopping take them to Greenwood Park where they can enjoy the playground, mini-railway and boat pond. This is another place which should not be visited at night.

National Botanical Gardens

Less than an hour's walk (4 km) from town on the city limits off Fifth Street Extension. Open dawn to dusk. The Gardens will appeal to those with a botanical bent or simply to those who enjoy a quiet walk. They include most of the 750 indigenous vegetation species plus a collection of plants from elsewhere in Africa. The Zimbabwean version of Kew Gardens covers 58 ha and offers fine opportunities for picnicking. Amateur botanists are welcome to consult botanical experts at the National Herbarium; phone (14) 72–5313/70–2236 to make an appointment.

Macgregor Geological Museum

Between Fourth and Fifth streets. Open weekdays. Of interest to gemmologists who will be able to discover where different types of rocks and gemstones are to be found in Zimbabwe.

National Handicraft Centre

Corner Grant and Chinhoyi streets in the southern part of the city near the Mbare market. Open Monday to Saturday 09:30 to 17:00. The centre displays a wide range of handicrafts from all over Zimbabwe. For more on crafts and sculpture see page 70.

Places of interest outside Harare

Heroes' Acre

Take the Bulawayo road and travel for 7 km from the city centre to the west of Harare. You need to obtain permission from the Ministry of Information at Linquenda House in Baker Avenue (usually available while you wait) to visit this 57 ha burial ground for those that fought in the struggle for independence.

The imposing memorial is a national monument to the men and women who have been declared national heroes.

Mukuvisi woodlands

Take the Mutare road and turn right at Glenara Avenue. This is the headquarters of the Zimbabwe Wildlife Society, which also runs a gift shop that is open from 09:30 to 16:00 daily (Tel 73-1596).

Just 6 km outside Harare in the southern suburb of Hillside, this is a small pocket of wilderness (265 ha) where visitors can view a number of species of wildlife (elephant, wildebeest, zebra, rhino, duiker and steenbok) from a game viewing platform and also undertake a guided tour on foot. This isolated patch of indigenous woodland is also a haven for birds. Safaris on foot last two hours and start on Wednesday at 14:00, Saturday at 14:30 and on Sunday at 08:30 and 14:00.

Chapungu Kraal

Doon Estate, 1 Harrow Road, Msasa, Beverley East, off the Mutare road, Tel Harare 4-7533/4-7472. About 8 km from the city centre along the Mutare road. Here visitors can watch traditional tribal dance displays at weekends (dances are on Saturday at 15:00 and Sunday at 11:00 and 15:00). Also stroll in the modern sculpture garden which houses an impressive collection of verdite and soapstone sculptures. The 5 ha complex also boasts a traditional 19th century Shona village with its own resident N'anga or traditional healer.

Each Wednesday night from 18:00 to 22:30 the sculpture park is open to visitors for a barbeque and dance performance by torchlight. It is essential to book.

Epworth balancing rocks

Travel 12 km east along Manica Road. Although a number of routes leaving Harare have balancing rocks along them, these are the most spectacular concentration of balancing rocks, weathered into unusual shapes by millenia of erosion.

Domboshawa rock paintings

From town take Seventh Street, which becomes Chancellor Avenue then the Borrowdale road and eventually the Domboshawa road, for 25 km and turn right at sign.

These Bushman (San) rock paintings are not in good condition, having fallen victim to the ravages of time and man. Visit the interpretation centre to get the most out of what you see. Note also the interesting granite formations.

Lake Chivero (formerly Lake McIlwaine)

Head out on the Bulawayo/Gweru road for about 35 km. This artificial dam, which provides Harare's water supply, offers water sport (the north bank) and peaceful seclusion and access to wildlife (the south bank).

The northern resort area features Admiral's Cabin, which has a swimming pool and boat hire, the Hunyani Hills Hotel – a good stop-off for tea, and the Sailing Club. You can spend the night either at the Hunyani Hills Hotel or at the nearby National Parks campsite. See Accommodation, page 143.

The southern part of the lake and game park are home to rhino, antelope, zebra, giraffe and more than 200 species of birds (see Bird-watching, page 68.)

If you can ride, try hiring a horse from the Parks office and tour the park on horseback with a guide. It beats being on foot or in a car.

Ewanrigg Botanical Gardens

About 35 km north-east of Harare on the Enterprise road. The trip takes about half an hour by car; watch out for the Ewanrigg signpost.

The 285-ha landscaped gardens are most noted for their ancient cycads, colourful aloes and cactuses from all over the world, so go in the dry mid-winter season when they are in splendid bloom. Also visit the herbarium and water garden. The gardens have plenty of picnic spots and barbecuing areas.

Larvon Bird Gardens

Take the Bulawayo road and travel for 17 km. Open Monday to Friday (except Thursday) 11:00 to 17:00, weekends 09:00 to 17:00.

The gardens house some 400 species of indigenous and exotic birds in very agreeable surroundings. They are well worth a visit by the whole family, as children can enjoy themselves in a play area while their parents have tea and scones to the accompaniment of soothing bird noises.

Snake park

At the 14 km peg on the Bulawayo road, Tel (14) 76-2526. Open from 08:00 to 17:00. Designed to appeal to those who are fascinated by these intriguing reptiles, the snake park features some of Africa's most dangerous specimens.

Lion and cheetah park

On the Bulawayo road 23 km from Harare. Open daily from 09:00 to 17:00. Telephone Norton (162) 2-7567/69/64. Half of this privately owned park is a drive-through area where animals such as giraffe, sable, elephant, wildebeest, impala and even crocodile roam freely, while the other half is more zoo-like. The main attractions are of course the lions, leopards and cheetah. The lions are said to have "played" bit parts in a number of films, including *King Solomon's Mines*. It is worthwhile visiting the park at feeding time, generally in the late afternoon. Refreshments and curios are available.

BULAWAYO

Dominating the south-western portion of the country, Bulawayo is Zimbabwe's second largest city with a population of about half a million people. Set in mining and ranching country, it also plays a major role in the industrial and commercial activity of Zimbabwe.

Bulawayo is the capital of Matabeleland province, while Harare is the capital of Mashonaland. The different people, styles and language which predominate in the more southerly city give it a completely different feel to the capital.

Where to go 19

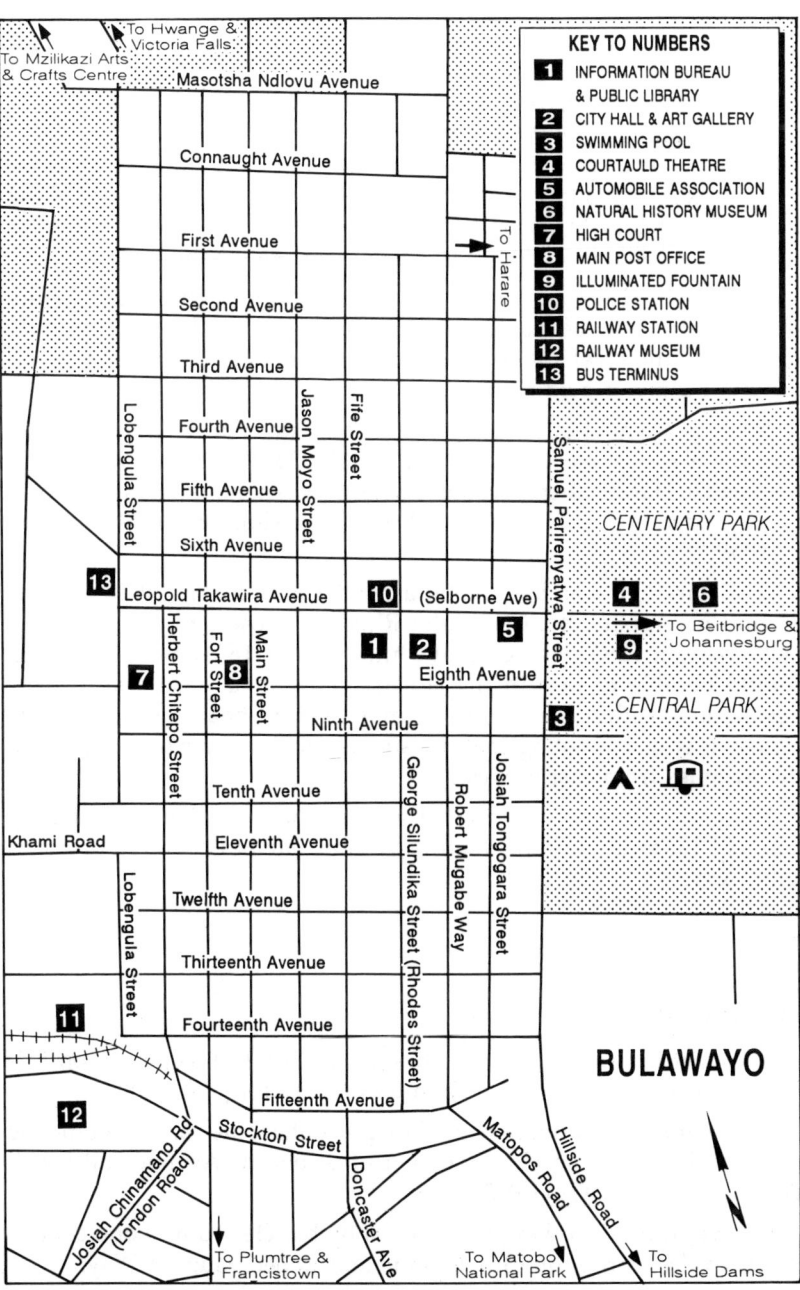

Like much of Zimbabwe, the place seems to be stuck in a time warp focused on the 1950s and '60s. The blame or, depending on how you see it, the credit, for this could be given to the shortage of foreign exchange during the 1960s and '70s – during the sanctions-plagued UDI years. The impact of that era, and the continuing squeeze on foreign exchange allocations, means that little from the outside world has had a chance to make its mark on Zimbabwean life. Witness the old cars and slightly dated dress of most of the inhabitants.

Founded in 1894 on one of the reigning chief Lobengula's kraals, Bulawayo's name means "place of slaughter" in Sindebele. The name referred to the chief's military victories. In its day, Bulawayo was the centre of a minor gold rush.

There is a school of thought which maintains that Bulawayo lost its rightful place as the dominant city of Zimbabwe, a role which was assigned to Harare, then Salisbury, when it was nominated as the capital of the Federation of Northern and Southern Rhodesia and Nyasaland in 1959.

Like Harare, it was built along a regular grid, making it easy to get around in. Apparently, Cecil John Rhodes, whose forces took control of the city in 1893, insisted that a full team of 16 oxen and a wagon should be able to turn in the streets, hence their great width. Most destinations within the city are at most half an hour's walk from the centre. It is worth noting that the streets run from north to south and the avenues from east to west.

The city centre is concentrated around the City Hall, bounded by Leopold Takawira Avenue, Eighth Avenue, Fife Street and Robert Mugabe Way.

Tourist information

The Tourist Information Bureau lies in the City Hall complex, on Fife Street between Eighth and Selborne avenues, Tel (19) 6–0867.

For motoring information and maps contact the AA (Automobile Association) at Fanum House, corner of Selbourne Avenue and Josiah Tongogara Street, Tel (19) 7–0063.

A novel way of viewing the town is by bicycle. To hire one contact Royal Cycles, corner of 13th Avenue and Robert Mugabe Way.

Access

By road
Bulawayo is well placed at the conjunction of the Beitbridge/Harare Road and Victoria Falls/Masvingo roads.

By air
The city is well served by air links with daily scheduled flights to Harare, Johannesburg and Victoria Falls. Each flight is met by the Air Zimbabwe bus (terminus in town at the Bulawayo Sun Hotel).

By train
Bulawayo serves as the main railway junction for Zimbabwe linking Harare, Gaborone, Gweru and Victoria Falls.

Distances
Bulawayo –
Harare:	440 km
Beitbridge:	326 km
Victoria Falls:	439 km
Masvingo:	280 km
Nyanga:	684 km

Accommodation and restaurants
See Chapter 7 for details. Note that the top-of-the-range hotels expect payment in foreign currency or that you produce a bank receipt for money that has been changed to the equivalent amount.

Places of interest in Bulawayo

National Natural History Museum
Situated in Centenary Park, on the corner of Leopold Takawira Avenue and Park Road. The museum is open daily including Sundays and public holidays (except Christmas Day and Good Friday) from 09:00 to 17:00. The museum, the eighth largest of its kind in the world, is said to have the largest mammal collection in Africa. One of the first of the staggering 75 000 exhibits you will see is the huge stuffed elephant standing nearly 3,5 m at the shoulder, supposedly the second largest example in the world. The museum has been rated as first-class, even better than its capital city counterpart. It is certainly worth a visit even for those who do not ordinarily enjoy visiting museums.

Railway Museum

In the south-west corner of the city, just south of the railway station between Customs and Prospect avenues. Open Tuesday to Friday 09:30 to noon and 14:00 to 16:00 and Sundays 12:00 to 17:00. The museum features rolling stock and steam engines, Rhodes' private coach and an assortment of railway machinery from the last century. Although steam enthusiasts should not miss it, they may be disappointed by the lack of detailed background information. There is also a display illustrating the history of railway transport in Zimbabwe.

Zimbabwe's need to conserve foreign exchange coupled with its plentiful coal supplies, have ensured that Zimbabwe has some of the world's few remaining steam locomotives. Nearly 100 of these old workhorses still ply the tracks. (See page 78 for information on rail safaris.)

Art Gallery

Corner of Robert Mugabe Way (Grey Street) and Leopold Takawira Avenue (Selbourne Avenue). Open daily from 10:00 to 17:00 except Monday and Saturday afternoons. Small but worth a quick visit for its cultural artefacts and local painting exhibits.

Jairos Jiri shop

Situated in the grounds of the Bulawayo City Hall on the corner of Selborne Avenue and Robert Mugabe Way. This rewarding craft shop is run by the disabled as part of a nationwide welfare co-operative project. Its merchandise includes wall hangings, lampshades, table cloths, basketry, beadwork, pottery, sisal matting and soapstone carvings.

Mzilikazi art and craft centre

Mzilikazi suburb, 4 km to the north-west of the city. Open from 08:30 to 12:30 and 14:00 to 16:00 on weekdays, Tel (19) 6-7245. This non-profit cultural centre features pottery, sisal basketry, art and sculpture. The work of craftsmen who trained here is now known internationally. Note that its products are available countrywide.

Centenary Park

With Central Park it flanks Leopold Takawira Avenue, the main entrance to Bulawayo's central business district. A 45-ha park with its own lake, small game park, mini-railway and aviary. Just 10 minutes' walk from the city centre, it will particularly appeal to those with children, who will especially enjoy the elegant fountain just across the road.

Central Park

On the opposite side of the road from Centenary Park on Leopold Takawira Avenue. Another peaceful haven where you can while away the hours on a hot summer's day. Central Park has a caravan park and campsite as well as a very elegant fountain that presents a spectacular fairytale sight when it is illuminated at night.

Places of interest outside Bulawayo

Khame ruins

Situated 22 km from city centre. Take Main Street in a westerly direction. Visit the small museum first, which will help you make some sense of what you see. Also known as "Khami", the ruins represent the remains of a city-state established in the 17th century (after the demise of the Great Zimbabwe civilisation), which lasted around 200 years before it was destroyed by fire. The ruins are linked in terms of the dry-stone building technique with Great Zimbabwe. In fact, Khame is the second largest and most important site after Great Zimbabwe.

After the fire, the power base moved to Dhlodhlo (see below). For those with an archeological bent, there are still many ruins visible that feature terraces and passages.

Dhlodhlo/Danangombe ruins

On the road between Bulawayo and Gweru to the north – about an hour and a half's drive from Bulawayo. Follow road to Gweru till just after the town of Shangani, turn right at the signs, and continue for 22 km. These ruins will interest mostly those who are keen on archeology.

Naletale ruins

Follow same route as above to Shangani and continue 25 km from turnoff to village. More attractive and interesting than the Dhlodhlo ruins, but much smaller. It also has good views.

Cyrene Mission

About 32 km from town on the road to Botswana, take left turning at Cyrene road. Religious murals cover many walls at this Anglican mission featuring the school of art introduced in 1939 by Canon Edward Patterson. Also on view is ornately carved furniture produced by the pupils, whose education is based on the tenets of self-sufficiency, art, farming and building. The mission is rated as a national treasure house.

Matobo National Park

See page 37.

Tshabalala Sanctuary

Travel 8 km south of the city centre, off the Matobo road. Open from 06:00 to 18:00. The sanctuary has a variety of antelope, zebra, giraffe, wildebeest and tsessebe and kudu. Visitors are able to walk or ride in the sanctuary, which is run by National Parks.

Chipangali Wildlife Trust

Travel 23 km south of Bulawayo on Beitbridge road. Closed every Monday and Christmas Day. The sanctuary houses sick, abandoned and orphaned wild animals including birds, and is likely to appeal to all animal lovers.

NATIONAL PARKS

Zimbabwe's national parks are listed below in alphabetical order. The parks' addresses and locations are provided together with the main attractions of the park, how to get there, when is the best time to go, accommodation and special precautions.

If you require more detailed information, contact either the Department of National Parks and Wildlife Management, Central Reservations Office, Travel Centre, Jason Moyo Avenue, Harare, or P.O. Box 8151 Causeway, or Tel (14) 70–6077, from Monday to Friday 07:45 to 16:15, or the Wildlife Society of Zimbabwe, Wildlife Centre, Mukuvisi woodlands, Glenara Avenue South, Hillside, Harare, P.O. Box 3497, Harare, Tel (14) 73–1596.

Bush etiquette

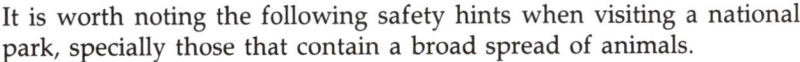

It is worth noting the following safety hints when visiting a national park, specially those that contain a broad spread of animals.

- Female elephants with calves spell trouble. Never get too close or ever try to separate them as they are acutely protective.

- Lions are at their most aggressive when mating so be sure to never disturb them. Otherwise lions are aggressive when hungry or when guarding kills and their young, so never provoke them unduly in such situations. If you come across one on foot, don't run away in fear if you can help it for this might provoke the chase response. Your best bet is to back off slowly, as calmly as you can, avoiding eye contact. This advice also applies to encounters with leopards.

- Be wary of walking on river banks in the early morning or late afternoon. You might come across a hippo on its way to or from the water, depending on what time of the day it is. When this happens hippos feel threatened and can be extremely aggressive.

- It's best to wear dun or fawn coloured clothes to blend in with the bush, and avoid bright, light colours unless you particularly want to be noticed. Note that it is illegal for civilians to wear camouflage gear. Note also that tsetse flies and mosquitos are said to favour people wearing dark colours.

- Be especially careful about bringing fruit into national parks. The smell of strong-smelling fruit, and oranges in particular, can cause an elephant to attempt forceful entry into your car and certainly attract baboons and monkeys who are not above trying to break into your tent or chalet. Beware leaving anything that might attract hyenas, who have been known to eat hosepipes, tin cans, shoes and the like. Make sure your rubbish is properly disposed of.

- Never approach any wild animal, no matter how docile it appears to be. The buffalo, which usually looks so cow-like, can be a real killer when aroused.

Chimanimani National Park

(See also section on hiking, page 62.) Private Bag 2063, Chimanimani, Tel (126) 0–3322. For booking and other information contact National Parks office in Harare, see page 155.

26 Zimbabwe

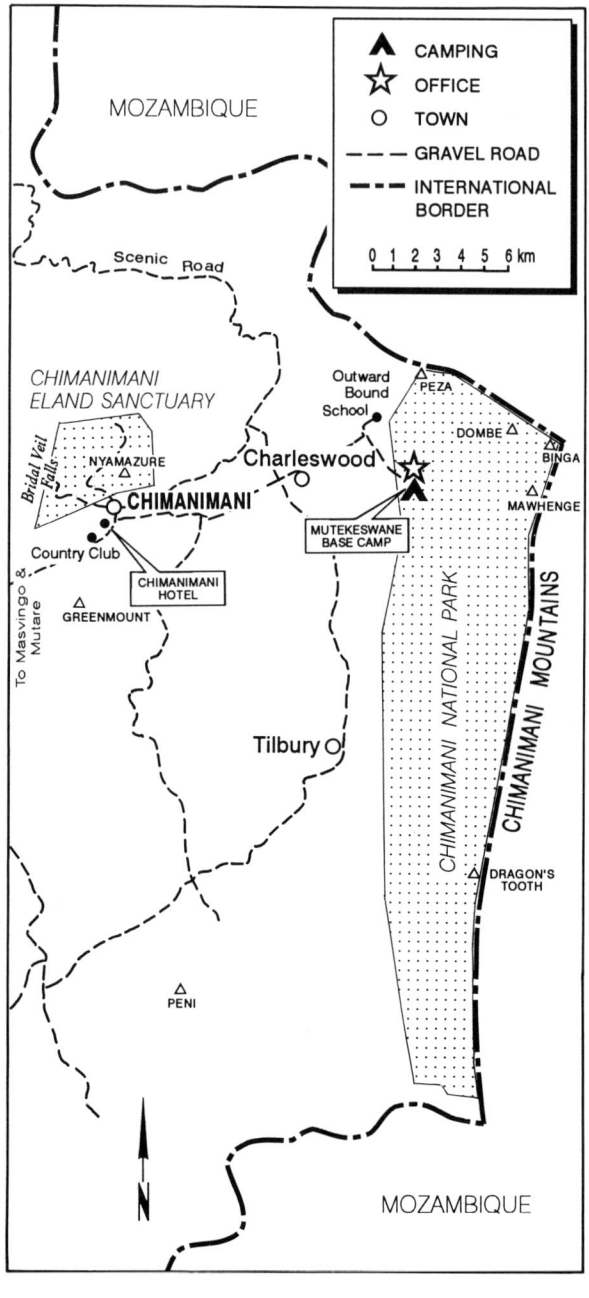

Where is it?

The park straddles Zimbabwe's eastern border with Mozambique. Its point of access from Zimbabwe is at the foot of the mountains 21 km from Chimanimani town. There are no roads in the park – hiking is the only way of getting around.

Small and mountainous, the park is only 171 km^2 in extent. It's best to get hold of the Ordnance Survey Map (1:50000 Melsetter 1932 D4 and 1933 C1 and C3 from the Surveyor General's office, Harare; Electra House, Samora Machel Avenue, Harare, P.O. Box 8099, Causeway, Harare, Tel (14) 79–4545) before entering the park. Keep well clear of the border as there is guerrilla activity in neighbouring Mozambique.

Why go there?

Particularly good for hiking enthusiasts as the park is accessible only on foot. It is unspoilt and there are few signs of human influence. The park's sandstone and quartzite rock formations present a refreshingly different aspect from the more rounded granite formations found in other parts of Zimbabwe.

Rivers, waterfall and pools, gorges and spectacular peaks help to provide varied interest while climbers will enjoy reaching Peza (2 179 m) and Binga (2 440 m) peaks, both of which have outstanding views. There is also something for the botanically inclined: cedar and yellow-wood trees, giant tree strelizias, cycads, ferns, heathers and helichrysums, orchids and aloes.

Animals that have been seen here include bushbuck, sable, eland, blue duiker, klipspringer and leopard.

If you prefer to see national parks from the comfort of your car and can't really call yourself a hiker, it is not worth your while travelling to this far-flung corner of Zimbabwe, which takes a relatively long time to get to by car.

Other attractions in the area

The Bridal Veil falls and the Eland Sanctuary, which are both close to Chimanimani village.

How to get there

See route three, page 115. Off the A9 coming either from Mutare or Masvingo to Chimanimani village. From there take 21 km of gravel road to base camp Mutekeswane, which has a car park, ablution and information facilities.

Distances

Chimanimani National Park –

Chimanimani village:	19 km
Mutare:	169 km
Masvingo:	297 km
Harare:	432 km
Bulawayo:	582 km

There are no roads in the park, only footpaths.

When's the best time to go?

Try to avoid the height of the rainy season if possible, otherwise you will have to contend with cloudy and misty conditions.

Where to stay

You can camp anywhere in the park including Mutekeswane base camp, or stay in the mountain refuge hut overlooking the Bundi Valley. This is a two to three hour walk from Mutekeswane, depending on your level of fitness. A number of caves within the park provide shelter, including Terry's cave, Red cave, North cave, Peterhouse cave and Digby's cave.

For accommodation outside the park see page 138.

Special precautions

Bring all your own supplies. Make sure you are well prepared for the trip by contacting the Mountain Club of Zimbabwe, P.O. Box 1945, Harare.

Chizarira National Park

For accommodation and other information contact National Parks in Harare, see page 155.

Where is it?
Set between the A1 and A8 main roads south of Lake Kariba, the nearly 2 000-km² Chizarira is too remote and inaccessible for the average tourist.

Whether you come from east or west, you'll have more than six hours of travelling to do on dirt roads, and although a four-wheel drive vehicle is not strictly necessary in the dry season, it could make life somewhat easier. The closest store and fuel supply are at Binga which is some 90 km away.

Distances
Chizarira National Park –

Harare:	504 km (via Karoi)
Hwange:	209 km (via Gwayi)
Victoria Falls:	313 km (via Gwayi)
Bulawayo:	372 km (via Gwayi)
Binga:	90 km

Why go there?
You can undertake a guided tour, using your own transport, with the assistance of the national parks' guides or you can take a walk with an armed guide for a very reasonable fee.

This park is noted more for its untouched and varied scenery than for large concentrations of animals. However, the park is home to the threatened black rhino, a wide range of antelope, lions, leopards, some 12 000 elephants, cheetah, roan antelope, tsessebe, reedbuck, duiker, impala, sable and eland.

When's the best time to go?
Outside the rainy season, say between June and October, as roads are impassable during the rains.

Where to stay
At one of three exclusive camps: Mabolo Bush Camp on the Mucheni River with few facilities (i.e. bring your own tent and don't expect running water); Busi Bush Camp, with some rudimentary sleeping facilities, and Kasiwi, situated on the Lusilukulu River, with the best facilities. Kasiwi and Mucheni are both 6 km from the park headquarters at Manzituba. Book through National Park central reservations in Harare.

Special precautions
You need special permission from the provincial warden to enter. Enquire about the procedure when making your booking through National Parks central office, Harare.

Gonarezhou National Park

Private Bag 7003 Chiredzi, Tel (131) 2980. For booking and information contact National Parks central office in Harare, page 155.

Where is it?

Zimbabwe's second largest game park is sprawled over 5 000 km^2 in the south-east corner of the country in the heart of the hot, semi-arid lowveld (150–400 m above sea level). The park receives few visitors, because of the possibility of incursions by poachers and guerrillas from neighbouring Mozambique. Large sections of the park have been closed to visitors for many years and are unlikely to open unless the security situation in Mozambique improves substantially. At present only Zimbabwean citizens and their guests may visit the park. To be sure of the current regulations ask central reservations which sections are open to the public.

Why go there?

The park has one of only two populations of nyala antelope in Zimbabwe, the rare knee-high suni antelope and the striped king cheetah. The red sandstone Chilojo cliffs, visible for 50 km, are a sight to remember, especially when their colour is enhanced at sunrise or sunset.

Most of the park has dry lowveld vegetation interrupted by the major riverine belts of the Save and Runde rivers. The name "Gonarezhou" means "Elephant refuge" as the park has the reputation for being home to some very large elephant, made rather antagonistic by poaching. The famous Chilojo cliffs are difficult to get to without four-wheel drive. Over 400 species of birds have been recorded in the park.

How to get there

From Masvingo head south on the A4 to Ngundu. Take the A10 to Chiredzi and continue 20 km past the town. Turn right onto a dirt road that bypasses Chipinda Pools and crosses the bridge on the Runde River. Follow the national park signs on the road which leads to Mbalauta and Swimuwimi camp in the south of the park.

Distances

Park reception –
    Chiredzi: 55 km
    Masvingo: 260 km
    Bulawayo: 540 km
    Harare: 560 km
    Beitbridge: 320 km

When's the best time to go?
The park is open only during the dry season, from May to October.

Where to stay
The two main camps are Swimuwimi (with chalets) and Mbalauta (five caravan/camping sites). Swimuwimi is 8 km from the warden's office, Mbalauta only 600 m. There are a number of other basic campsites, all set along the banks of the Runde River. For accommodation outside the park see page 140.

Special precautions
You will need prior written permission to enter the park so don't just turn up. It is essential to book in advance through National Parks central reservations. Bring all your own supplies as no fuel or stores are available inside the park. Take appropriate anti-malaria precautions as Gonarezhou lies in an endemic malarial area. The nearest hospital is in Chiredzi.

Hwange National Park
Private Bag DT5776, Dete, Tel Dete (118) 64. For booking and information contact National Parks in Harare, page 155.

Where is it?
Lying in the western sector of Zimbabwe, along the border with Botswana, Hwange comprises over 14 000 km^2 of bush scrub adjacent to the Kalahari Desert. It is Zimbabwe's largest and most famous game park. Only the extreme eastern edge has been developed.

Why go there?
Known to be the best wildlife preserve in Zimbabwe – as one wit put it: "wall-to-wall animals". There are so many elephants (over 20 000) that they need to be culled annually as the park cannot sustain higher numbers. The large animal population, varied vegetation, good roads and well-equipped camps make Hwange (or "Wankie" as it used to be called) a popular destination for tourists visiting Zimbabwe.

The best places to see the animals are from the game-viewing platforms which have been erected at some of the waterholes, of which Nyamandhlovu is the most popular.

Game drives can be easily organised either from the park's reception office or the Hwange Safari Lodge, which lies outside the park. Game trails on foot are led twice a day by skilled and informative game scouts. These give you a real taste of what it is like to be in the wild, setting even the bravest heart aflutter. Asked if he had ever had to use his gun in the ten years he had been escorting walks, one game-guide answered: "Only once, when we came upon lions mating. Lions are at their most aggressive when mating". However, all he needed to do was fire his gun in the air and that managed to scare the lion off.

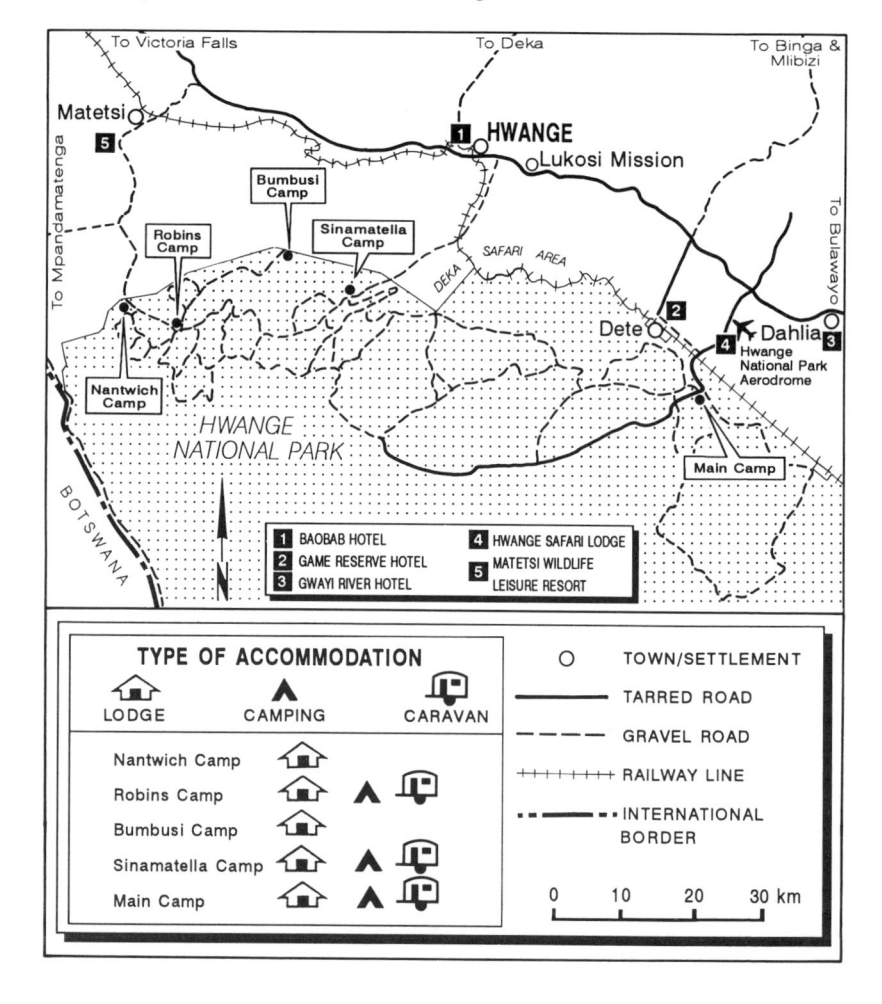

How to get there
Very accessible off the Bulawayo/Victoria Falls Road.
Distances
Hwange National Park (Main camp)–
Bulawayo:	267 km
Victoria Falls:	194 km
Beitbridge:	589 km
Harare:	704 km
Hwange town:	90 km

When's the best time to go?
From about August to late October which constitutes the late dry season, although it is open all year. As with any game, the best time to view is in the cooler parts of the day at dawn and dusk. Expect temperatures in the mid-30s during the dry season just before the rains, which usually start in early November. The temperature drops sharply at night, however.

In the early part of the dry season the grass is likely to be long, impeding visibility somewhat. During the rains, some of the 450 km of roads may have restricted access. It's best to check in advance with park authorities. The park is not at its best during December and May unless you want to view birds only.

Where to stay
See Accommodation, page 144 for details on private accommodation.

Main Camp, which also doubles as the main administrative headquarters for the park, is linked by tar with the main Bulawayo/Victoria Falls Road.

Sinamatella Camp is situated some distance away to the north-west, on a plateau overlooking a large plain famous for its elephant, while at Robins Camp you are most likely to see lion. This also applies to Nantwich Camp, which overlooks a waterhole, but which is in a more isolated area. Accommodation is in lodges, exclusive camps and campsites.

Even though it is advisable to book in advance, you can take a chance and just turn up. You may be asked to wait till 17:30 to take a booking that has not been claimed.

Outside the park is Hwange Safari Lodge, which is privately run and is a very popular option, as is Sikumi Tree Lodge.

Lake Chivero National Park

(Formerly Lake McIlwaine National Park) Private Bag 962, Norton, Tel (162) 2329 between 07:00 and 18:00. For booking and information contact National Parks central office in Harare, page 155.

Where is it?

Lying some 40 km to the south-west of Harare, it is just the right distance away to be popular as a day or weekend retreat for Harare residents. It is also very accessible along the main Bulawayo Road.

The lake constitutes Harare's principal supply of water.

What's there to see?

In the southern part of the park you'll see rhino, antelope, giraffe, zebra and a good selection of birds. There are also rock paintings at Bushman's Point and Crocodile Rock. If you like horse riding, you can explore the park on horseback. Rides must be booked either for early morning or mid-afternoon.

How to get there

Drive down the Bulawayo road from Harare and watch for the signs.
Lake Chivero –
Harare:	40 km
Bulawayo:	397 km

When's the best time to go?

In springtime when the vegetation is particularly appealing and the unfurling leaves of the msasa tree with their autumnal colours deceive visitors from the northern hemisphere into thinking that autumn has arrived.

Where to stay

Chalets or more private lodges can be booked through National Parks central booking office. For accommodation nearby consult page 143.

Mana Pools National Park

Private Bag 2061, Karoi. For booking of accommodation contact the National Parks central reservations office in Harare, page 155.

Where is it?

Mana Pools National Park flanks the Zambezi River for part of its journey through a shallow valley filled with islands and sandbanks and pools formed when old river channels cut off from the main flow were filled up with water. The river runs through the national park for a distance of 50 km. The park covers an area of 2 000 km^2.

Why go there?

To view abundant wildlife in a natural and very attractive habitat. You also have the option of gameviewing by canoe safari (see page 66). Unesco has judged the area to be so attractive and unusual that it has nominated it a World Heritage Site. This means that its fauna and flora are afforded extra protection and the number of visitors is strictly limited and controlled. Note that it is possible to walk without a guide within the park.

Elephant, buffalo, impala, zebra, waterbuck, lion, wild dog, leopard, black rhino, nyala, eland, kudu, hippo and of course crocodile are abundant. Mana's superb birdlife includes more than 350 species.

How to get there

Travelling from Harare, Makuti is the last place where you can obtain petrol before turning off to Marongora (some 16 km further). Always make sure you reach Marongora before 15:30 so that you can obtain the required entry permit, because it could take two hours or more to cover the 74 km from the entrance to Nyamepi Camp if you travel at the prescribed speed of 40 km/h.

Distances

Mana Pools (Nyamepi Camp) –

Harare:	400 km (six hours)
Bulawayo:	837 km
Beitbridge:	979 km
Kariba:	172 km
Chirundu:	113 km

36   Zimbabwe

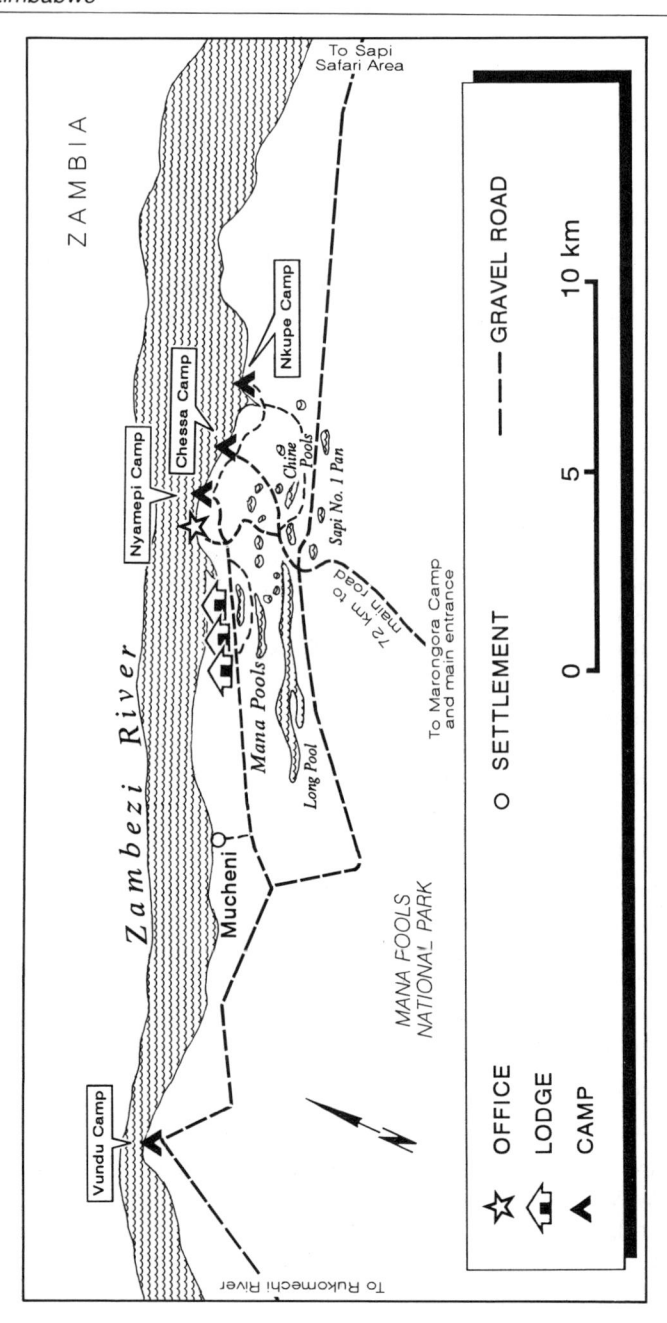

When's the best time to go?

During the dry season when the animals are forced to come to the pools and especially the late dry season during October. Avoid the school holiday period in August/September. The park is closed during the rainy season, November to April.

Where to stay

The Mana campsites are Nyamepi and Mucheni, Nkupe, Old Tree Lodge and Vundu, which are all on the Zambezi River. There are also private camps, Ruckomechi and Chikwenya. See Accommodation section, page 149.

Special precautions

Watch out for tsetse fly, wild animals, malaria and bilharzia. Book well in advance as accommodation is very limited and the park is popular. It is not permitted to bring oranges or other strong smelling fruit into the park as this might attract elephants too closely.

Matobo National Park

Private Bag K5142, Bulawayo, Tel Matobo (183-8) 0-1913. At a future date the number will change to (183-8) 2504. A dash in the dialling code indicates that you must wait for a second dialling tone. For booking accommodation, contact National Parks central reservations in Harare, see address page 155.

Where is it?

The park is situated some 32 km to the south of Bulawayo.

How to get there

Follow the Matobo road from Bulawayo for 32 km.

Distances

From the Matobo entry point to –

Bulawayo:	32 km
Harare:	469 km
Beitbridge:	354 km
Kariba:	711 km
Chirundu:	694 km

Zimbabwe

Why go there?

This rock garden of the giants is richer in high-quality rock paintings and strange granite formations than animal species, although the more interesting species present include the white rhino and the largest concentration of black eagles anywhere, as well as a number of giraffe, sable, impala, zebra, kudu, bushbuck, leopards, baboons and klipspringer. Like clouds, the strange rock formations lend themselves to fantasy images, from which you can read all kinds of shapes and structures.

It is certainly worth visiting "World's View", the awe-inspiring site of Cecil John Rhodes' grave, a place where time seems to stand still. World's View also has the distinction of being a religious shrine and repository of ancestral spirits. In ironic contrast to this imposing grandeur is the local keeper's Monty Pythonesque lizard feeding routine. Three times a day (or more if you ask him) a wide array of multi-hued lizards gather to be fed by hand. The lizards frenetically jump, scramble and climb for their reward of small mouthfuls of *sadza* (cooked stiff maize meal porridge).

Another must is a visit to the white rhino shelter. Visitors can also go for walks or horse rides in the vicinity of Maleme Dam.

When's the best time to go?

It's better to go during the drier parts of the year otherwise rains may cause minor road problems, especially on the way to Maleme Dam.

Where to stay

A tonic for the eye after all the boulders is the tranquil Maleme Dam, where the park's accommodation facilities (see page 158) are situated. These include chalets, cottages and lodges which should be booked in advance. The Black Eagle and Fish Eagle lodges have particularly good views.

Matusadona National Park

For booking and information contact National Parks central office in Harare, see address page 155.

Where is it?

On the southern shore of Lake Kariba. Most easily reached by boat. The southernmost two-thirds of the park comprises inaccessible (except on foot) steep escarpment and undulating plateau, while the northernmost third is made up of relatively flat Zambezi valley floor bounded by the lakeshore. It is nearly 1 500 km^2 in extent, bounded in the west by the Ume River and in the east by the Sanyati Gorge.

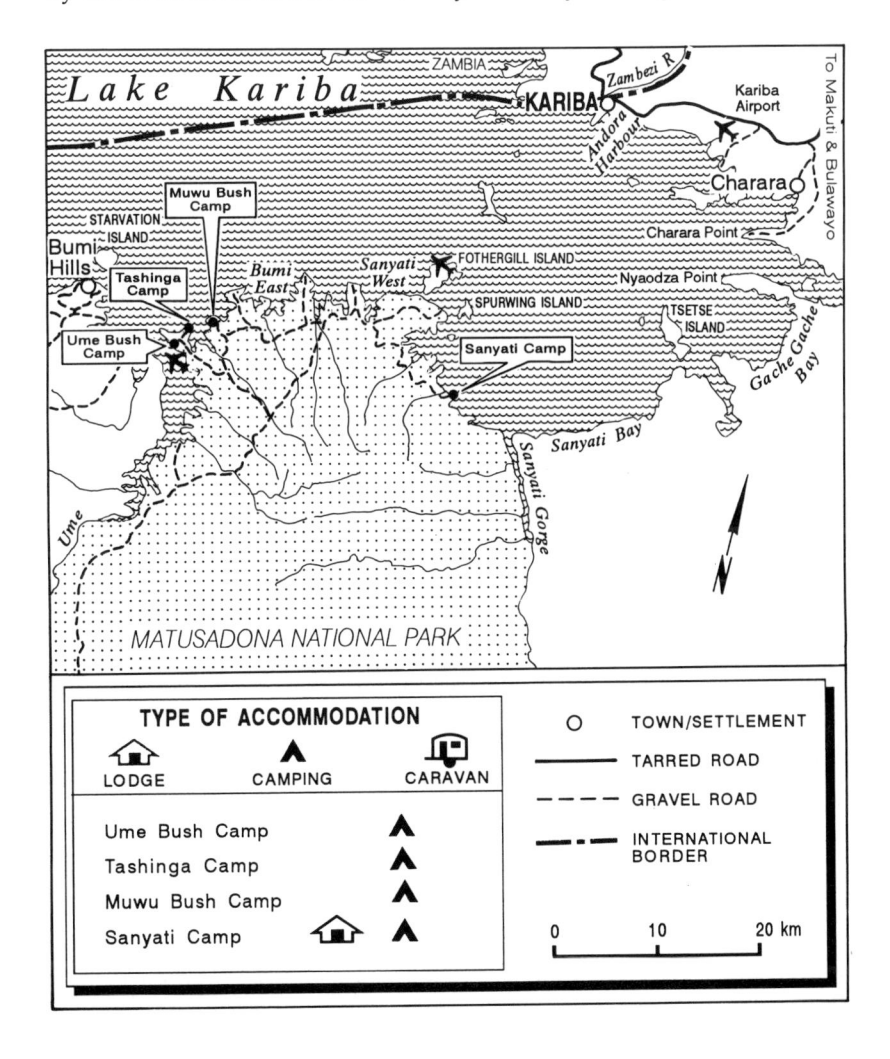

Zimbabwe

Why go there?

For superb tiger fishing opportunities, and walking in the company of a game guide only.

The park is home to black rhino, plenty of elephant and buffalo, antelope such as sable and roan, kudu, eland, waterbuck, hippo, plentiful lion, impala, hyena, crocodile, leopard and more than 400 species of birds.

How to get there

By boat: Catch the not very comfortable weekly DDF ferry (see page 53) from Andorra Harbour at Kariba to Tashinga, which it stops at on its run to Bumi Hills. Or hire a boat from Kariba. Private craft can be moored at Sanyati and Tashinga campsites.

By road: The journey is not really worth it unless you are determined. Drive from Harare north to Karoi, head west at Karoi on gravel road for approximately 150 km, then turn off to park through Chifudze gate. It is almost essential to use a four-wheel drive vehicle.

By air: Tashinga has an airstrip and places on flights can be obtained at Kariba.

When's the best time to go?

September to October, especially if you want to fish, for the International Tiger Fishing Contest is held then. Otherwise it is open all year.

Where to stay

Two camps on the Lake; Sanyati, the smaller camp in the east near the mouth of the Sanyati Gorge, and Tashinga in the west which constitutes the camp headquarters; there are also three exclusive camps catering for small parties on the Ume River, bookable through National Parks. Commercial photo-safari camps are situated on Spurwing and Fothergill islands with superb views of the Matusadona mountains. The Bumi Hills Hotel overlooks the lake to the west of the park and offers guests a water wilderness safari. See Accommodation, page 147.

Special precautions

Unless you are booked to join a safari package outfit, you must bring all your own provisions, including fuel.

Mtarazi National Park

For booking and information contact National Parks central office in Harare, see address page 155.

Where is it?
In the east of the country on the southern border of Nyanga National Park.

Why go there?
It is much less developed than Nyanga, offering dramatic and varied scenery that will attract hikers in particular. Pungwe Gorge and Falls is a must, as well as the 760 m drop of the spectacular Mtarazi Falls, the highest in Zimbabwe. Botany lovers will enjoy the montane vegetation which includes a huge variety of ferns, many orchids, many flowering trees as well as the slow-growing hardwoods.

See Hiking, page 62.

How to get there
From Rhodes Camp in the Nyanga National Park, follow directions to the Scenic Road which provides access to the most popular viewpoints such as Pungwe Falls and the Gorge as well as the Mtarazi Falls and the view into the Honde Valley below. Alternatively, if you are travelling from Mutare heading north to Nyanga, you can turn off from the main road, once you reach the vicinity of the Nyanga National Park, and follow the signposts to the Scenic Road.

To get to the top of Mtarazi falls, it is a good walk from the car park off the Scenic Road.

When's the best time to go?
Avoid the height of the wet season as visibility and hiking access may be impeded.

Where to stay
There are no official campsites within the park, but at Pungwe Drift there are two superbly situated National Parks lodges.

Nyanga National Park

Private Bag T7901, Mutare, Tel Nyanga (129-8) 27-4384. A dash in the dialling code indicates that you must wait for a second dialling tone. For booking and information contact National Parks central office in Harare, see address page 155.

Where is it?

In the extreme east of the country. Covering just under 300 km^2 on the Mozambique border, the park ranges in altitude from 880 m to 2 300 m.

Why go there?

To enjoy dramatic highland scenery, cool green forest, tumbling waterfalls and cascades, abundant trout fishing and walking opportunities. There is no big game, just some small mammals and antelope. Hikers will enjoy hiking in the southern sector of the park and climbing Mount Nyangani, Zimbabwe's highest mountain at 2 593 m. The Ziwa ruins might interest history buffs.

How to get there

From Harare head south-east from the city centre following signposts to Marondera and Nyanga. From Mutare, head due north on the main Mutare/Harare road. From Bulawayo, head either for Harare and then change direction to the east for Nyanga or head due east via Masvingo, then changing direction for Mutare and Nyanga.

Distances

Nyanga National Park –
Harare:	258 km
Mutare:	105 km
Masvingo:	392 km
Beitbridge:	680 km
Bulawayo:	672 km

When's the best time to go?

From April/May to August and September when it is dry and warm. The wetter part of the year can be quite miserable for fairly long spells. Altitude makes it colder than lower-lying areas so in June/July it is at

Where to go 43

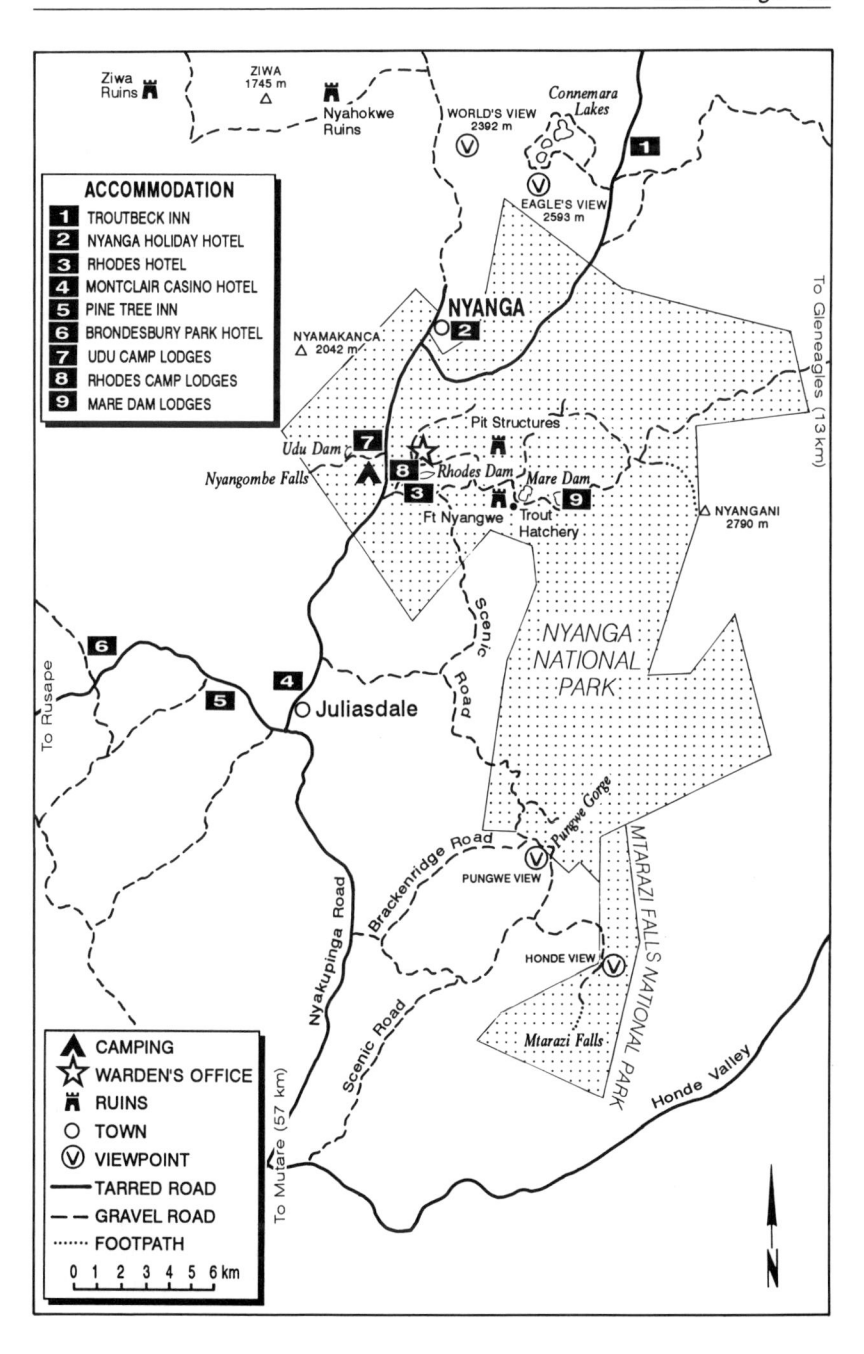

its coldest. Always bring warm clothing for the freezing cold temperatures at night.

Where to stay
The most convenient places to stay are the extremely reasonable Rhodes Camp and Udu Camp nearest to the main entrance, and the Mare Camp lodges. You can also camp. See pages 151–2 and 159 for details of accommodation. The privately run Rhodes Nyanga Hotel is also a good option. Bring provisions with you if you are not staying in the hotel.

Victoria Falls National Park
(See also Victoria Falls, page 57.) Private Bag 5925, Victoria Falls, Tel (113) 4310/4222. For booking and information contact National Parks central office in Harare, see address page 155.

Where is it?
At the extreme north-west point of Zimbabwe. The national park includes the Falls and immediate surrounds, covering an area of 23 km^2.

Why go there?
Mostly to see the spectacular, mile-wide Zambezi River pouring over a 100 m cliff. Otherwise, the very much secondary attraction is the rainforest and all the attendant vegetation such as palms, ferns, mosses, creepers, mahogany and ebony trees, the exotic puffball plant and a few animals such as warthog, antelope, baboons, waterbuck, bushbuck and vervet monkeys. The birdlife is superb.

How to get there
From Victoria Falls town head towards the falls and border post. You will see the entrance on the left. You will need to park your car on the right of the road and walk into the falls area along a footpath that takes you past the various falls. If you wish to go on foot from town it is a short walk but in October and November the heat can make it quite exhausting.

When's the best time to go?
Early morning and late afternoon for optimal light conditions. Being there around sunset is also extremely rewarding. Make enquiries if you are in the area at the time of the full moon as the park opens so that

Where to go 45

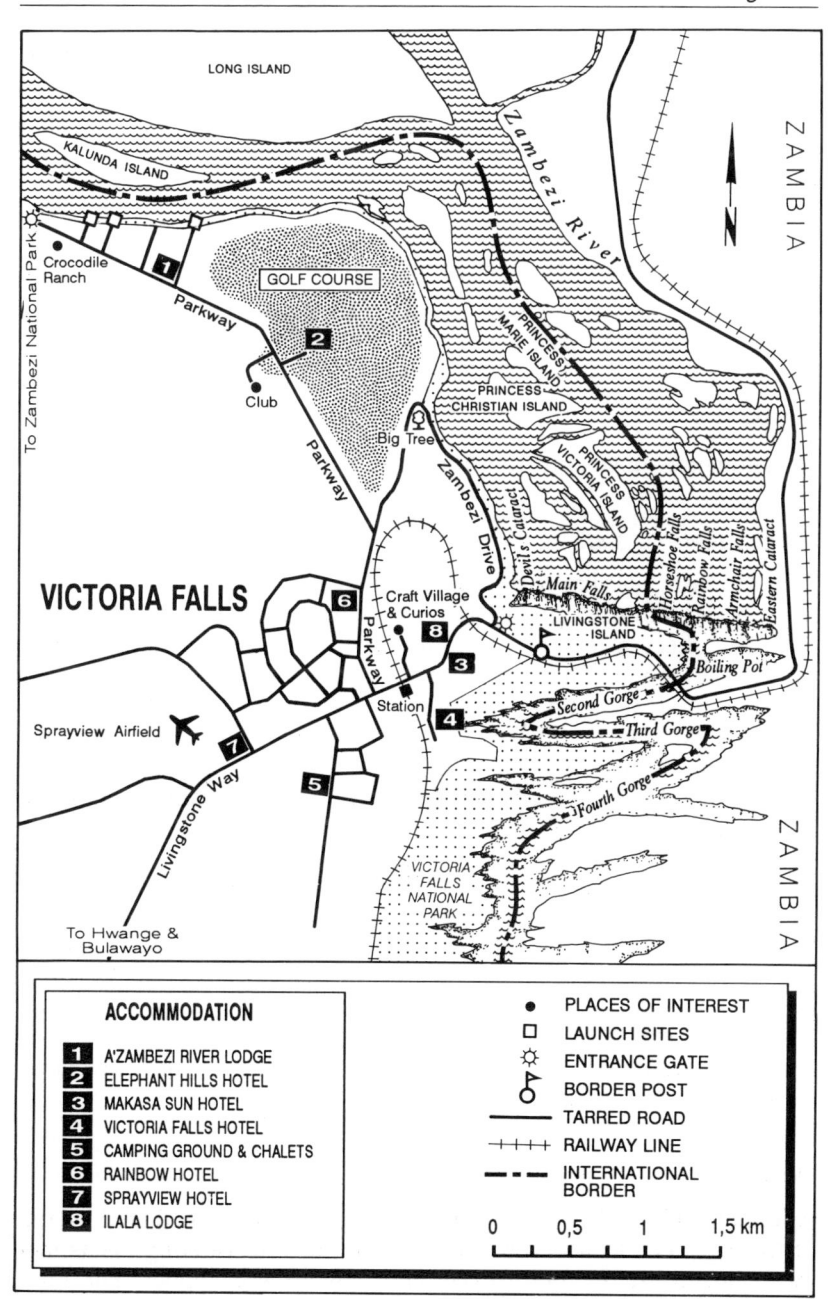

VICTORIA FALLS

ACCOMMODATION	
1	A'ZAMBEZI RIVER LODGE
2	ELEPHANT HILLS HOTEL
3	MAKASA SUN HOTEL
4	VICTORIA FALLS HOTEL
5	CAMPING GROUND & CHALETS
6	RAINBOW HOTEL
7	SPRAYVIEW HOTEL
8	ILALA LODGE

- • PLACES OF INTEREST
- □ LAUNCH SITES
- ☼ ENTRANCE GATE
- ⚲ BORDER POST
- —— TARRED ROAD
- ++++ RAILWAY LINE
- —·— INTERNATIONAL BORDER

0   0,5   1   1,5 km

visitors can view the lunar rainbow. During the dry season the Falls are at their least spectacular and you will hardly get wet while viewing them from the rainforest. At the end of the rains in April or May, the view of the falls will be obscured by the increased spray thrown up by the huge volume of water.

Zambezi National Park

For booking and information contact National Parks central office in Harare, see address page 155.

Where is it?

Six kilometres upstream from the Falls and Victoria Falls town.

What's there to see?

This smallish, 560 km^2 park contains antelope, including sable, monkeys, birds, rhinos, elephant, lion, zebra, hippo, giraffe and even leopard. The sheer extent of the Zambezi River with its islets, islands, sandbanks and riverine forest and the usually steamy temperatures combine to create a unique atmosphere that has changed little since the great explorer David Livingstone first saw it. The surrounding infrastructure of posh hotels and a bustling town catering to a thriving tourist market lies discreetly some distance from the main action of the Falls and the river.

How to get there?

From Victoria Falls town follow the signposts from the town centre.

When's the best time to go?

Any time outside the wet season as the park is closed from November to April.

Where to stay

Approximately 20 self-catering lodges are privately situated on the bank of the Zambezi. Unless you want to have all your catering needs met by staying in a hotel, these are certainly a worthwhile option. For those who want to immerse themselves in a fishing holiday, several self-catering fishing camps have been established on the banks of the Zambezi within the park's boundaries. See accommodation, pages 152–4 and 159.

GREAT ZIMBABWE

The name "Zimbabwe" is said to be derived from the Shona word for "stone house". The ruins are spread out over several square kilometres and the more you explore them the more you appreciate the awesome task that lay before the mysterious builders of the Rozvi empire's citadels. Unlike most of the structures in Africa, which are not built to last, Great Zimbabwe was strong and solidly constructed. It has lasted more than 700 years, and it is the biggest of the over 100 "zimbabwes" to be found throughout the country. It is also the largest ancient man-made building in Africa south of the Sahara.

Despite its strength and permanence, no mortar was used in its construction, just the drystone technique. Each block of stone was cut to size, a task that must have taken much effort, time and skill, considering the primitive types of tools at the disposal of the Shona in the Middle Ages.

To date, mystery still surrounds the occupants of Great Zimbabwe and how their downfall came about. The complex was built to accommodate up to 30 000 citizens between the thirteenth and fifteenth centuries. Many myths have arisen about it, linking the complex with ancient and exotic civilisations, stories of King Solomon's mines and the Queen of Sheba, trade with the seafaring Portuguese, the Egyptians and the Indians.

To do this World Heritage and National Monument site proper justice, you will need about four hours to explore. If you go in summer, restrict your visit to the early hours of the day or even to late afternoon when it is cooler.

Most tourists wander around the Grand Enclosure and some might wish to tackle the steep walk to the "Acropolis" on the hill. It pays to visit the small museum at the entrance (open 08:00 to 17:00) to purchase Peter Garlake's illuminating book: *Great Zimbabwe Described and Explained* and also *Life at Great Zimbabwe*, a smaller pamphlet aimed at schoolchildren but nevertheless very worthwhile. These will explain the ruins and their significance in much greater detail.

The museum also houses the Zimbabwe soapstone birds of unknown species, which you may have noticed on Zimbabwe's coat of arms, flag and currency. Just over a foot high, the birds are thought to have adorned the tops of pillars around the site. The museum also displays a number of iron tools, ornaments and jewellery dating back to the time of inhabitation of Great Zimbabwe.

The best view of the Great Zimbabwe site and further afield to Lake Mutirikwi (formerly Lake Kyle) is from the hill complex, so go there first to appreciate the enormous scale of the place.

In brief, there are three main walled complexes spread over some several hundred hectares. These comprise the Hill complex, the Valley enclosure and the Great Enclosure. The Hill complex is thought to be the oldest, and is accessible via the Ancient or Modern ascents, both of which start near the craft shop.

The Great Enclosure from where the Rozvi royalty ruled within a number of enclosed courtyards, is sited appropriately at the foot of the hill that dominates the area and contains the much-photographed nearly 10 m high Conical Tower monument.

The Great Enclosure is surrounded by a massive wall which is 5,2 m thick in parts, 250 m long and nearly 11 m high. The walls feature intricate geometric chevron, herringbone, chequer, cord and dentelle patterns. Contained within the enclosure is a complex system of passages, stairs and chambers, said to have segregated the inhabitants according to power, class and status.

Great Zimbabwe is said to have been "discovered" by a German hunter in 1871. The ruins were first investigated archeologically in 1905.

Much controversy followed with two camps supporting opposing views, one being that a foreign race was responsible for the ruins, and the other that a totally indigenous race had built them. Current archeological consensus is that Shona tribesmen built Great Zimbabwe.

Theories suppose that the complex supported prosperous dynasties whose wealth derived from catttle. Overpopulation and crowding is thought to have brought about the collapse of the powerful state, and offshoots began to develop in the west at Khame (south of Bulawayo) and to the north at Naletale and Danangombe.

How to get there

Great Zimbabwe is situated in south-east Zimbabwe, 28 km south of Masvingo. Follow the signposts as you leave town.

Distances

Masvingo –
Harare:	292 km
Bulawayo:	280 km
Beitbridge:	288 km
Nyanga:	402 km

Where to stay

At Great Zimbabwe Hotel, at the campsite beneath the ruins, two resorts on Lake Mutirikwi, some 7 km away, or two hotels in Masvingo itself, 28 km away.

When's the best time to go?

Any time of year, but better in the early morning or late afternoon for better sunlight for photographers, cooler walking and fewer people, although the place isn't usually overcrowded. The ruins are open at 06:00 and close at 18:00 although the museum hours are from 08:00 to 17:00.

LAKE KARIBA AND ITS SHORELINE

Lake Kariba

Before the third largest man-made dam in Africa (after the Aswan Dam in Egypt and Cahora Bassa in neighbouring Mozambique) was built in the late 1950s, the area now under water was part of the sweltering Zambezi Valley.

During the flooding of the area after the dam was built many animals were drowned and those that survived were moved or trekked to refuge on higher ground including what is now the Matusadona National Park (see page 38). The rescue operation, during which some 5 000 animals were saved, was called "Operation Noah" and was led by Rupert Fothergill, a conservationist.

The valley was also the home of the Batonga people, some of whom had to be resettled on the southern portion of the lakeshore. Although an entire ecosystem was destroyed, a completely new one has been created and among Kariba's drowned forests, on its islands, in its bays, inlets and coves, and on sandy beaches crocodiles, hippo, scores of birds and abundant fish are to be found.

50 Zimbabwe

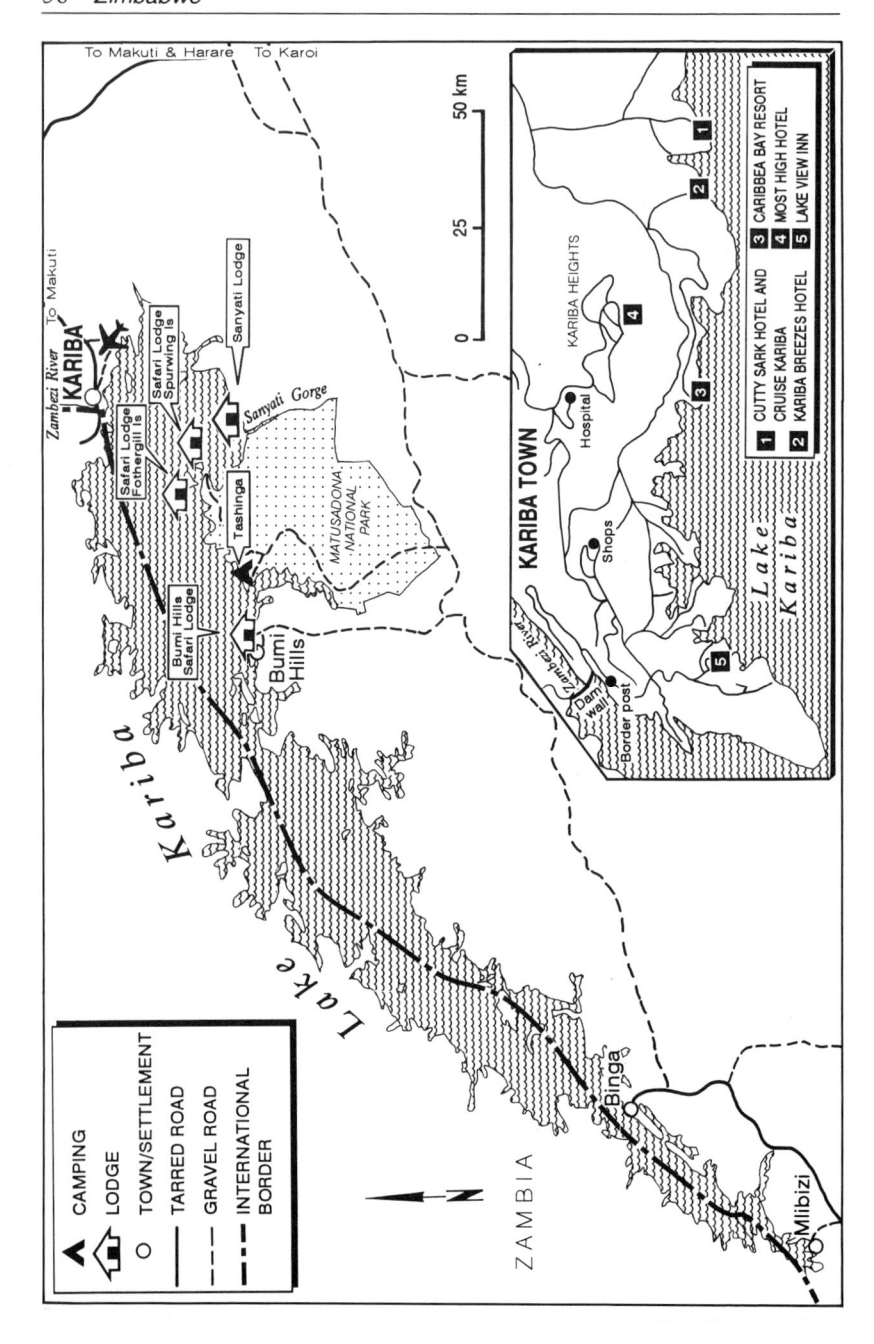

Physical statistics

The name "Kariba" comes from the Shona word *Kariwa* which means a little trap or bridge and refers to the narrow Kariba Gorge. The amazing engineering feat was completed in 1958. The dam wall is 128 m in height and has six floodgates which when open release 455 million litres of water per minute. Lake Kariba is 290 km in length and 42 km at its widest point. It is on average 18 m deep and covers a total area of 5 000 km². Ten thousand men toiled and 87 lost their lives in the construction of the 579 m-long dam wall which forms a bridge between Zambia and Zimbabwe. Those who wish to visit the dam wall need to apply for clearance at Zimbabwe customs. This is readily obtainable if you bring a passport with you. Photography of the wall is strictly controlled. Be sure to read the notices.

The dam was built to harness the waters of the mighty Zambezi in order to generate hydroelectric power. However, in the last ten years the waters of Kariba have been receding rapidly as a result of the drought experienced in the region. If you stay at one of the lakeshore hotels you may notice jetties standing many metres above the present level of the water. This will indiate to what extent the water level has dropped. This is another reason why the floodgates of the dam have not been opened for many years now.

The lake has changed a lot more than the lives of the Batonga who used to live on the land now covered by water. It is now a major recreational retreat for Zimbabweans and tourists from all over the world, who visit it to indulge in water sports such as yachting, waterskiing and fishing. It is also a haven for those who want to observe the many wild animals who are attracted to this giant watering hole.

Unless you enjoy high temperatures (often above 40 °C before the rains) and humidity, it's best to avoid high summer between December and February and rather visit in autumn (April/May) or spring (September/October).

There are three risks you must take into account if you do decide to embark on an intimate exploration of the lake – those of bilharzia, malaria and crocodiles. Residents who reckon they can outmanoeuvre the crocs, combat the bilharzia risk by regularly taking bilharzia treatment tablets, a procedure that might be questionable in the long run.

Kariba town

The "town" of Kariba constitutes the settlement at the top of the 600 m-high Kariba Heights, part of an area covering seven hills that overlooks the lake. The area was originally established by dam construction executives in their search for cooler temperatures.

There is not much to do at the town itself except take in the magnificent view over the lake, bargain with the ladies selling crochet work, who individually whisper their prices to you so that their competitors are kept in the dark, or stock up on groceries at the small supermarket (closed Wednesday afternoons). Otherwise, your best bet is to head for the resorts, take in a cruise or flight over the lake or try your luck at the casino at the Caribbea Bay complex. Other places to visit are the Church of St Barbara, a curved structure reminiscent of the dam's shape, dedicated to those who built the wall, many of whom were Italian, and particularly those who died during its construction. On your way down the old elephant track on which the tarred road was built, look out for the elephant that still wander over the hills in search of succulent snacks, especially just before the rains.

Visit the observation point for a superb view of the dam wall. The observation point also has a craft shop and the office of the Kariba publicity bureau.

Further down on the water is Kariba's harbour of Andorra, the terminus for the *Sealion* ferry, where luxury cruisers rub hulls with workmanlike fishing vessels.

Getting from Kariba to Victoria Falls or vice versa

There are a number of ways of doing this. You can fly either by private charter or national carrier. You can go on a private cruise which will start/end either at Mlibizi (three hours from Victoria Falls by road) or Binga (even further) or Kariba. Or you can take one of the two ferries run by DDF or Kariba Ferries (see addresses below).

Going by car is another option and there are three routes between Kariba and Victoria Falls. The longest one is via Harare and Bulawayo – a journey of 1 244 km. The route across the area to the south of the lake is considerably shorter although road conditions are poor and it would certainly take much longer. It is not a route that is normally used if one wants to get from Kariba to Victoria Falls.

The shortest and possibly most convenient route is that which links Kariba and Victoria Falls through Zambia. It is a journey of some 400 km on tar. If you have any South Africans or non-Commonwealth citizens in your party, they must have entry visas for Zambia and Zimbabwe to undertake this journey. Although it is said that you can sometimes obtain these at the border posts, it is wiser to plan ahead and obtain multiple-entry visas at the diplomatic offices in Harare or in your home country.

Accommodation
See pages 146–8.

Cruises
At 16:30 every day, UTC organises sundowner cruises which can be booked and boarded at Cutty Sark, Lake View Inn or Caribbea Bay.

Lake Safaris, Tel Kariba (161) 2474 and Cruise Kariba (161) 2697 both offer full-day game-viewing cruises to Fothergill Island.

Kariba Ferries, P.O. Box 578 Harare, Tel Harare (14) 6–5476 or Kariba (161) 2475 run a ferry between Kariba and Mlibizi in the extreme west of the lake. Sailing frequencies are irregular and if you wish to book your car on the ferry for the 22-hour one-way trip, you must contact them well in advance to check on ferry sailings.

You can also try the government-run DDF (District Development Fund) Shipping Services Ferry P.O. Box 195 Kariba, Tel (161) 2349/2694.

(See also Boat transport page 125).

How to get there
Kariba –
Harare:	366 km
Victoria Falls:	1 244 km by road
Bulawayo:	806 km
Makuti:	74 km
Beitbridge:	948 km
Nyanga:	637 km

There are daily air links with Harare, Victoria Falls and Hwange. There is no direct link between the airport and Kariba town but there are UTC (United Touring Company) connections with the various resorts as well as taxis.

Spurwing Island
Spurwing Island, just north of the Matusadona lakeshore, consists of a luxury tented camp with chalets and cabins under thatch that can

accommodate 40 guests at a time. Activities offered include game viewing, fishing, swimming in the camp's pool, walks, canoeing and boat hire. The camp offers superb views of the Matusadona Mountains and Sanyati Gorge. The camp is 40 minutes from Kariba by boat.

Fothergill Island

Also offers guided game viewing by safari boat, vehicle and on foot as well as tiger fishing in the Sanyati Gorge. The establishment consists of thatched lodges built on an unusual open design incorporating tree platforms. It was named after Rupert Fothergill, the game ranger who helped save over 5 000 animals when the dam was built by moving them to higher ground. The lake level has dropped so much in recent years that the island is no longer completely detached from the mainland.

Bumi Hills

The Safari Lodge offers luxury accommodation on houseboats on which a slow trip at your own steam is highly recommended.

Sanyati Gorge

Game viewing, birdlife, tiger fishing, 12 km of sharp-sided valley, only accessible by boat.

Binga

This is a settlement established around a small harbour on the western shore of the lake with caravan park, campsite and restcamp. The village also offers restaurant and basic shopping facilities, petrol, a crocodile farm and holiday chalets. Binga rest camp, Tel (115) 244, has a swimming pool filled with hot spring water.

Mlibizi

The ferry terminus at the western end of the lake, features a rest camp, campsite, chalets, shop and bottle store. Fishing is the main attraction, as the area does not offer much in the way of game viewing.

Important addresses and telephone numbers at Kariba

Hospital (161) 2382
Police (161) 2444

Breakdown service (161) 2919 or a/h 2918
Barclays Bank (161) 2303/2304
Air Zimbabwe (161) 2913

Air charter

United Air Charters (Pvt) Ltd. offers sightseeing flights, lake transfers and private charters. P.O. Box 93 Kariba, Tel (161) 2305. Note that the airport is a fair distance from Kariba and walking between the two is not recommended as you may be attacked by wild animals.

Boat charter

Anchorage Marina
Tel (161) 2245/2246.
Blue Water Charters (Pvt) Ltd.
Tel (161) 2971.
DDF Shipping Service: Passenger, Vehicle and Cargo carrying throughout the lake
P.O. Box 195 Kariba, Tel (161) 2694.
Kariba Cruises
P.O. Box 186 Kariba, Tel (161) 2839.
Kariba Ferries
P.O. Box 70 Kariba, Tel (161) 2460 or for booking Tel Harare (14) 6-5476/6-7661.
Lake Charters (Pvt) Ltd., game viewing and fishing charters
P.O. Box 70 Kariba, Tel (161) 2460.

Car hire

Avis Rent-a-car
Tel (161) 2555.
Hertz Rent-a-car   Lake View Inn
                   Tel (161) 2662.
                   Cutty Sark Hotel
                   Tel (161) 2321.
                   Caribbea Bay Hotel
                   Tel (161) 2454.

Safaris and tours

Buffalo Safaris and Zambezi Canoeing
Tel (161) 2827/2645 P.O. Box 113 Kariba.
Cruise Kariba (Pvt) Ltd
P.O. Box 1 Kariba, Tel (161) 2697.

Kazungula Safaris
P/Bag 2081 Kariba, Tel (161) 2253.
Shearwater Canoeing Safaris
Tel (161) 2345.
Chris Worden Safaris
Tel 2839 (personalised photographic and walking safaris),
P.O. Box 221 Kariba.
Kariba Safaris
Tel (161) 2554.
Lake Safaris
Tel (161) 2752, P.O. Box 34 Kariba.
United Touring Company, Caribbea Bay Hotel,
Tel (161) 2454.
Cutty Sark Hotel
Tel (161) 2321
Lake View Inn
Tel (161) 2662.

Hotels (see also Accommodation, pages 146–8)

***Bumi Hills Safari Lodge**
P.O. Box 41 Kariba, Tel (161) 2353.

Caribbea Bay
P.O. Box 120 Kariba, Tel (161) 2453/4.

**Cutty Sark Hotel
P.O. Box 80 Kariba, Tel (161) 2321/2.

Fothergill Island
Private Bag 2081 Kariba, Tel (161) 2253 or Harare (14) 70–5040.

Kariba Breezes Hotel
P.O. Box 3 Kariba, Tel (161) 2433/4.

**Lake View Inn
P.O. Box 100 Kariba, Tel 2411/2.

Mlibizi Safari Lodge
P.O. Box 298 Hwange, Tel Harare (14) 70-7072.

Most High Hotel
P.O. Box 88 Kariba, Tel (161) 2964.

Spurwing Island
Private Bag 101 Kariba, Tel (161) 2466.

VICTORIA FALLS

Zimbabwe's most popular tourist attraction, Victoria Falls ranks as one of the world's seven natural wonders. Majestic, turbulent, splendid, thunderous, plunging, awesome, roaring, boiling, swirling, rainbow-bedecked – these are all words used to describe the falls which are set in what you would imagine, without ever having been there, to be typical David Livingstone country.

The fourth largest river in Africa, the Zambezi takes a 2 700-km trip to the sea. The river's source is in north-west Zambia, and the falls are almost at its half-way mark. They are ranked among the biggest falls in the world. They are not as high as Niagara Falls, but they are one and a half times as long and have the widest curtain of falling water in the world.

One of Zimbabwe's four World Heritage sites, the falls form part of the Victoria Falls National Park (see page 44) and are just 6 km downstream from the Zambezi National Park.

The two-million year old falls spill the waters of the Zambezi over a distance of 1 700 m. During April and May, when the river's flow is at its peak, an estimated 545 million litres of water per minute plunges over the falls at a speed of 160 km per hour and is then constricted into a gorge which is only 30 m wide. The awesome power of the water creates spray clouds almost 500 m high. The spray feeds the tropical rainforest adjacent to the First Gorge. From about January till June or July, it is worth bringing your umbrella or raincoat to avoid a soaking. *"Mosi oa Tunya"* – the smoke that thunders – was the name given to the falls by the tribesmen who brought David Livingstone here nearly 150 years ago.

He was the first white man to set eyes on the falls, while on his travels through central Africa during 1855. His words on seeing the falls have often been quoted: "Scenes so lovely must have been gazed upon by angels in their flight". He named the falls after his Queen, Victoria.

A bronze memorial has been erected to David Livingstone near the Devil's Cataract opposite Livingstone Island, where he first saw the falls.

Five separate falls in all have been created by the force of the water: the Devil's Cataract, Main Falls, Horseshoe Falls, Rainbow Falls and the Eastern Cataract. They range in height from 61 m to 108 m.

The Devil's Cataract is 30 m wide and 70 m high, followed by Main Falls, nearly a kilometre wide and 93 m high, which is next to the crescent-shaped Horseshoe falls, followed by the tallest falls, Rainbow Falls at 108 m high. At the end of the rainforest lies Danger Point, from where you can view the swirling, steaming Boiling Pot and the end point of the falls, the 101 m-high Eastern Cataract.

Further upstream there are four palm-strewn islands: Kandahar, Kalai – where Livingstone is said to have camped – Palm Island and Livingstone Island.

In the narrowest part of the Second Gorge below the falls a bridge suspended 111 m above the Zambezi River (when it is at low water) was built in 1905 as part of Cecil John Rhodes' envisaged Cape-to-Cairo link so that travellers could appreciate the roaring majesty of the falls. The bridge also forms part of the Zambia/Zimbabwe boundary. Since it was built it has been the venue for some high-level talks which have taken place on a train on the bridge. One of the talks concerned the former prime minister of South Africa, John Vorster, and Dr Kenneth Kaunda, former president of Zambia. The full splendour of the bridge is visible from the Victoria Falls Hotel.

The tourism potential of the falls was appreciated as early as 1904 when the first hotel was built. Today the Victoria Falls Hotel still stands on the same spot but has changed a great deal over the years (see page 154).

When to go

The falls are at their lowest and least spectacular just before the rains, in October/November. The smaller volume of water means less spray and mist and better views. If you visit when the river is full there is far more thunder and drama, but visibility is poorer. The falls are very impressive either way. The best plan is to visit the falls twice, when they are at their lowest and when they are at their highest.

As with most dramatic views, the best time of the day to visit is in the early morning or late afternoon when the softer sunlight is better angled for photographers.

If you are in the area at full moon inquire whether the Victoria Falls National Park will be open for visitors to view the lunar rainbow.

How to get there
Distances
Victoria Falls –
Harare:	878 km
Hwange town:	104 km
Bulawayo:	438 km
Nyanga:	1 143 km
Beitbridge:	760 km
Chirundu:	1 100 km (via Harare)
Plumtree:	538 km

There are daily connections from the other main centres to the Victoria Falls airport, which is some 23 km out of town. See routes between Kariba and Victoria Falls, pages 52 and 121. The train departs from the station daily at 17:30 for Bulawayo.

Where to stay
See page 152.

What's there to see
The town
Victoria Falls town is blossoming as a result of the sharp increase in tourism in recent years. The tourist now has a wide range of accommodation options to choose from and a number of activities to while away the time when not viewing the falls. These include opportunities to go fishing (see page 75), game trails in game reserves and the Zambezi National Park (page 65), horse riding, flying, boating and what is said to be the world's most thrilling experience in white water rafting from just below the Boiling Pot for a stretch of 23 km through 13 sets of grade 4 to 6 rapids. The gorges or low-water runs are graded 5, a trip not suggested for the fainthearted. Internationally, rapids are graded on a difficulty scale of 1–6, with a rating of 6 being regarded as unrunnable.

Even from the centre of Victoria Falls town you can hear the falls and see the spray. Visit the Craft Village, with resident witchdoctor and displays of traditional rural arts, and take in the African Spectacular which is performed nightly at the Victoria Falls Hotel. There is a host of curio shops and stalls selling wooden and soapstone carvings and crocheted bedspreads that could be passed off as family heirlooms.

Visit the "olde-worlde" Edwardian station which is the terminus for the romantic overnight Bulawayo/Victoria Falls trip, depositing tourists just metres from the front entrance of the Victoria Falls Hotel.

Also worth a visit is the giant baobab on Riverside Drive, which is between 1 000 and 1 500 years old, has a girth of 16 m and is 20 m high.

Visit Spencer's Creek Crocodile Ranch and nature sanctuary. The crocs range from hatchlings to the largest male at over 4,5 m long and weighing more than 470 kg. The ranch is open from 08:00 to 16:30 every day except Christmas Day. Visit the Victoria Falls Snake Park, where you can see Africa's most dangerous snakes including cobras, mambas, gaboon vipers at close range in complete safety. The park also has eels, turtles, tree monitors and chameleons. The snake park is on Adam Stander Drive behind the post office and is open daily except Sundays.

How to get around

You can hire a bicycle from Avis in Livingstone Way or Michael's Cycles in Parkway. Or, for a completely different viewpoint, try the Flight of Angels, a 15-minute flight in a light, twin-engined aircraft above the falls that gives you a superb bird's-eye-view perspective. The other flight alternative is the 30-minute Sprayview air safari, which takes in the falls and the surrounding terrain, giving you a better understanding of the area if you have only limited time to spend at Victoria Falls.

Various "booze" cruises upstream from the falls are offered by the different tour operators at different times of the day (try sunset). Some cruises travel 2 km upstream to Kandahar Island and Hippo Pool. These cruises provide good opportunities to view hippos, crocs and the occasional elephant or herd of antelope coming down to the water for an evening drink.

Hours of business

Shops: Monday to Friday 08:00 to 13:00 and 14:00 to 17:00.
Banks: Monday, Tuesday, Thursday and Friday 08:30 to 12:30; Wednesday 08:00 to 12 noon; Saturday 08:00 to 11:00.
Town surgery: Monday to Friday 07:30 to 16:00.

Chinotimbas Clinic: 24 hours.
Border post: 06:00 to 18:00.
Customs and immigration town office open Monday to Friday only 08:30 to 16:00.
Petrol stations: Monday to Thursday 06:30 to 18:30; Friday to Sunday 06:30 to 19:00.
Post office: Monday to Friday 08:30 to 16:00; Saturday 08:30 to 11:30.
Air Zimbabwe offices: Monday to Friday 08:00 to 13:00; Saturday 08:00 to 11:45.

3. WHAT TO DO

WALKING AND HIKING

If you wish to plan a walking/hiking/climbing holiday in Zimbabwe you need to define your priorities and then plan accordingly. Rather than going under your own steam it is worth making contact with those members of the Mountain Club of Zimbabwe who know the country's uplands really well.

Climbers, backpackers and hikers are welcome to attend their regular meets, which are usually held every weekend. If you write to P. O. Box 1945, Harare, explaining the type of climbing or hiking you wish to do, they could point you in the right direction. You could also try contacting some of their members by phone at Harare (14) 3–6599/79–2492/72–7703/73–3577/3–6708.

Good ordnance maps in the scale of 1:50 000 are available from the department of the Surveyor General, P. O. Box 8099, Harare, or at their outlet on the ground floor of Electra House, Samora Machel Avenue in Harare, Tel Harare (14) 79–4545.

The Eastern Highlands

These offer an entirely different experience from walking in game parks; mountain walking and hiking amidst cool, montane evergreen forest, conifers and wattle, spectacular waterfalls and rugged cliffs, with some relaxing trout fishing thrown in for a little diversion and welcome evening log fires. The best areas for climbing in the Eastern Highlands are at Nyanga and Chimanimani.

In the Nyanga area, a company called Trails Unlimited offers backpacking and riding excursions as well as mountain safaris on Mount Nyangani, Zimbabwe's highest peak. They can be contacted at P. O. Box 701 Mutare, Tel (120) 63–3094.

The Mountain Club of Zimbabwe has its own hut on Mount Nyangani which is a good morning's hike from the path that leaves from the car park. It tends to be wet and misty on the summit, as well as somewhat marshy in the wet season.

It is advised that you do not climb the mountain after 14:00 as the minimum time for climbing to the beacon and back is three hours. You are also advised not to climb if mist or cloud is visible round the summit. Children under the age of 10 are not allowed to climb while those between 10 and 17 must be accompanied by a responsible adult.

It is suggested that you report to the National Parks office or the police both before and after your planned climb. There are signs and markers up and down the mountain and these should be followed. If you do deviate from these markers and get lost, just remain where you are until help arrives.

Further south the Chimanimani Range, which straddles the border with Mozambique, contains peaks of up to 2 436 m. Part of the range lies within the Chimanimani National Park (see description, page 25). The park is very undeveloped and not at all commercial. There are no roads inside it, just tracks and footpaths. The area offers superb hill-walking and steeper climbing for the more intrepid. Note that there is no big game on the high ground, just some eland, sable and bushbuck. Occasionally you may encounter some elephant and buffalo in the densely forested valleys.

The park's base camp, Mutekeswane, is 21 km from Chimanimani and can be reached by gravel road. It has ablution facilities, an information office and car park. A main track leading up the mountains starts from here. You need to bring all your own provisions and can camp anywhere in the park, but remember to advise the warden first.

During the rainy season the area is prone to sudden storms, so it is wiser to go in the dry season, May to November.

Of the trails leading off from the main inner valley, one leads up 2 215-m Dombe peak, another to 2 179-m Peza peak and a third to Binga, 2 440 m. Botanists and bird lovers will particularly enjoy a ramble through the foothills. The unfurnished refuge hut is situated some 490 m above the base camp and overlooks the Bundi River. It can be reached in two or three hours depending on your level of fitness.

There are plenty of walks in Nyanga National Park, particularly through the areas containing the ancient ruins. If you are staying at Udu Camp, the Nyangombe Falls is a one and a half hour walk through the hills or half an hour by road. Ask at Udu Camp office for directions. Take extra care not to get too close to the falls, as the rocks are slippery and several people have fallen to their death here. From Troutbeck you can take a 7 km uphill walk to World's View along the dirt road that will take you past the Connemara lakeland.

Taking the Scenic Road from Rhodes Camp watch out for the signposted track to Pungwe Drift. Follow the track for about 45 minutes and then follow the path along the river for another 30 minutes before reaching the top section of the Pungwe Falls.

Walking safaris – national parks

Some of the parks offer guided walking safaris, sometimes lasting several days. These are designed to bring the visitor as close as possible to the wild. Other walks can be done without a guide. Remember that the presence of a guide does not guarantee safety. In the face of a charging elephant he has time to shoot once, maybe twice, and if he misses the results could be fatal. In fact the guides are not allowed to actually shoot to kill but must first fire a warning shot. This is in the hope that a charging animal will be so frightened by the warning shot that it will stop in its tracks. However, there have so far been hardly any such encounters on guided walks.

Some of these safaris are not luxury excursions and you are expected to provide your own food and equipment. Check with the organisers beforehand when making your booking. National Parks usually lead wilderness trail walks during the dry season only (May to November). Walks are restricted to those over the age of 16. You must bear in mind that you will need to carry all your own equipment, and as trails can take up to four days and cover difficult terrain, you will need to be reasonably fit. Guided walks lasting just a few hours are available in some of the parks for those who seek something a little less arduous.

Matusadona National Park

Backpackers Africa advertises a six-day hike only for those who are physically fit. Contact Shearwater Adventures P. O. Box 3691, Harare, Tel (14) 73–5712, Telex 26391.

National Parks offer wilderness trails from May to October. Lasting for four days they can begin either from Tashinga or Sanyati West. Contact the department of National Parks and Wildlife Management.

Kalambeza Safaris specialises in walking and game drives in Matusadona. P. O. Box 121 Victoria Falls, Tel (113) 4480/4451.

Victoria Falls

Backpackers Africa's foot or horseback safaris in Matetsi Safari Region last up to three days. You may also want to try the 10 km walk starting from Livingstone's statue opposite the falls following the riverside path to the A'Zambezi Lodge then further up along the road. Watch out for hippos.

Hwange

National Parks' wilderness trails start at Sinamatella and Robins camps and last three or four days. Two-hour guided walks are conducted from each camp at 06:00 and 17:00 each day depending on the weather. Book in advance.

Chizarira

National Parks' organised trails on foot take place during the winter and spring months of May to October.

Mana Pools

Wilderness trails offered by National Parks and Wildlife.

Matobo National Park

Walks through the granite hills will appeal to those who are interested in rock painting. Try a day-long hike to World's View (see description, page 38) and back, or you can take a full day to get to Toghwe Wilderness area and spend the night there in camp at either Toghwana or Mtsheleli Dams.

Mukuvisi woodlands (Harare)

This small nature reserve, very close to the centre of Harare, offers two-hour foot safaris through 168 ha of indigenous woodland stocked with rhino, elephant, wildebeest, antelope and zebra. The safaris leave on Saturday at 14:30 and Sunday at 08:30.

Further information can be obtained and all walks can be booked through National Parks central booking office, P. O. Box 8151 Causeway, Harare, Tel (14) 70–6077 or Bulawayo Booking Agency, P. O. Box 2283, Bulawayo, Tel (19) 6–3646.

WATERSPORT

Watersport enthusiasts will find Zimbabwe a paradise considering the country's warm climate, Lake Kariba, the Zambezi River and numerous large dams to which the public have access.

Boating/yachting

Most dams have facilities for boating – whether you hire boats or bring your own. If you want to plan a boating holiday your best bet is probably Lake Kariba where the main sailing season usually falls between April and September. Contact Kariba Yacht Safaris, c/o Percom Services, Tel Harare (14) 73–6789 or 79–0277. Cutty Sark Marina, P. O. Box 80 Kariba, can help if you fancy the idea of sailing a 22-foot yacht as part of a flotilla of up to five yachts. They offer various cruise packages suited to two adults and two children or four adults at a crush, lasting one to 14 days depending on how much sailing you want to do. Even if you have no experience you are given adequate instruction to enable you to sail the boat, bearing in mind that help is always at hand, if necessary. You could also try Kariba Cruises, P. O. Box 186 Kariba, Tel (161) 2839. A number of other companies offer cruises on boats where you are just a passenger and can sit back and relax, possibly combining the trip with some fishing or swimming in the middle of the lake where there is no bilharzia and supposedly no crocodiles.

Other major dams that cater for boating are Lake Chivero (formerly Lake McIlwaine) near Harare and Lake Mutirikwi (formerly Lake Kyle), very near Masvingo in the south of the country.

The following companies at Kariba offer boat hire/charters:
Anchorage Marina, P. O. Box 61 Kariba, Tel (161) 2245.
Blue Waters Charters, P. O. Box 78 Kariba, Tel (161) 2972.
Kariba Breezes Marina, P. O. Box 15 Kariba, Tel (161) 2475.
Kariba Yachts, Tel (161) 2321.
Lake Safaris, P. O. Box 34 Kariba, Tel (161) 2752.

Canoeing

A variety of canoeing safaris are offered on the Zambezi River from below the Victoria Falls in the extreme north-west of Zimbabwe to Kanyemba in the extreme north-east at the borders with Zambia and Mozambique. The stretch from Kariba to Kanyemba takes nine days. You can take in smaller stretches, e.g. that from Kariba to Chirundu (three days). This trip is not as exciting as other stretches, such as that from Kariba to Mana Pools, which lasts five or six days, or Chirundu to Mana Pools, lasting four days, or Mana to Kanyemba through the steep Mpata Gorge. Each stretch of water is controlled for traffic and only one party per day is allowed in a specific section. Canoes are usually of the Canadian type, made of fibreglass and 5,7 m in length, able to accommodate two people.

Canoe safari operators do not expect tourists to be experienced canoeists and generally provide a canoe guide who is unarmed but experienced and has a good knowledge of fauna and flora. When booking your trip ask whether the operator offers guided excursions inland from the river.

A canoe trip offers unparalleled game and birdwatching opportunities as you glide silently past the river bank. You are able to stop for meals, walks and swimming.

Watch out for heatstroke and sunburn in the hot summer months, from October to March. Probably the best time to go is in September before the heat really intensifies and as water reserves on land are drying up, compelling the thirsty animals to go to the river.

There are also canoe trails on Lake Kariba near Matusadona and Sanyati Gorge. See Fothergill below.

The following companies arrange Zambezi canoe safaris:
Backpackers Africa, c/o Safari Interlink, P. O. Box 5929 Harare, Tel (14) 72–0527.
Buffalo Safaris, P. O. Box 113 Kariba, Tel (161) 2645.
Chipembere Safaris, P. O. Box 9 Kariba, Tel Kariba (161) 2946.
Fothergill Island, Private Bag 2081 Kariba, Tel (161) 2253.
Goliath Safaris, P. O. Box CH 294, Chisipite, Harare, Tel (14) 70–8843.
Jacana Canoe Trails, P. O. Box 801 Harare.
Shearwater, 5th Floor Karigamombe Centre, Harare, Tel (14) 73–5712.
Zambezi Whitewater Safaris, P. O. Box 66293, Kopje, Harare, Tel (14) 70–2634.

White water rafting

The rapids just beyond Victoria Falls are said to offer the world's ultimate one-day white water rafting experience. Internationally, rapids are graded on a scale from 1–6. The Zambezi white river rafting course includes five rapids in the Grade 5 category which is the highest grade considered runnable. The run consists of 13 rapids interspersed with calmer waters over a distance of 23 km through the steep-sided Batoka Gorge. This adrenalin-pumping experience is offered by operators who run inflatables guided by trained raftsmen. At the end of the run you can't just climb in a car, heave a sigh of relief and drive home. You still have to complete the steep and strenuous 304 m climb out of the gorge.

Most operators stipulate that they will accept people between 16 and 60 on their packages, but the upper limit depends on the fitness and attitude of the participant. No experience is necessary as full instructions are provided.

All you need to take for one-day trips are sunglasses, string to hold them on, a swimming costume, suntan lotion, hat, t-shirt and shoes. On the longer trips, which can last up to seven days, your belongings will be transferred for you by vehicle between overnight stops.

The period around July/August is best for high water trips while the September to December/January period is ideal for low water trips. Subject to river levels, there are no trips during May or June.

You must book well in advance to be sure of getting on. The following operators organise lake/river boat trips:

Anchorage Marina, P. O. Box 61 Kariba, Tel (161) 2245.
Blue Waters Charters, P. O. Box 78 Kariba, Tel (161) 2971.
Kariba Breezes Marina, Box 15 Kariba, Tel (161) 2475.
Lake Safaris, P. O. Box 34 Kariba, Tel (161) 2474.
Rex Taylor, Kariba Yacht Safaris, Cutty Sark Marina, P. O. Box 80 Kariba, or 6 Fairfield Road, Hatfield, Harare, Tel (14) 5–0305.
Safari Interlink, P. O. Box 5929 Harare, Tel (14) 72–0527.
Shearwater Adventures, P. O. Box 3961 Harare, Tel (14) 73–5712.
Sobek Whitewater Adventures, P. O. Box 60957 Livingstone, Zambia, Tel (3) 2–1432. Packages usually include professional guides, food, transportation and safety equipment. Non-Zambian residents must pay in foreign currency.
Zambezi River Safaris, P. O. Box CH 69 Chisipite, Harare. Tel (14) 4–4045.

BIRDWATCHING

There are more than 600 species (640 including migrants and residents) to delight birdwatchers in Zimbabwe. About 75 of these are European migrants, while 60 are African migrants. Zimbabwean law affords special protection to over 40 species.

The best time to go in order to see the Palearctic migrants is during the months of January and February when the greatest variety of species is present. However, a number of the national parks are closed at this time because the rains make many of the roads impassable.

Most of the places on the usual tourist routes offer worthwhile bird-watching opportunities but there are several areas which are particularly rewarding.

The Eastern Highlands

These contain a number of species endemic to Zimbabwe at several locations, with the Vumba area near Mutare being the most rewarding.

Hwange National Park

Features a number of western species. Take particular note of the Kori bustard, which weighs up to 20 kg and is said to be the largest flying bird in the world.

Harare

The Mashonaland Bird Club, forming part of the Ornithological Association of Zimbabwe, holds regular outings. Contact them at P. O. Box 8382 Causeway, Harare, for further information.

The Larvon Bird Gardens are situated just 17 km from Harare on the Bulawayo Road. The gardens are open every day during the week (except Thursday) from 11:00 to 17:00 and on the weekends from 09:00 to 17:00.

Larvon features some 400 bird species and includes a natural lake which attracts a number of species of waterfowl.

To get to Mukuvisi woodlands, which is only 6 km outside Harare, follow the Mutare Road from Harare and turn right at Glenara Avenue. This isolated patch (168 ha) of indigenous woodland is a haven for birds. Foot safaris last two hours and are offered on Wednesdays at 14:00, Saturdays at 14:30 and Sundays at 08:30 and 14:00.

Lake Chivero (formerly McIlwaine), south-west of Harare, is home to several water and woodland species.

Bulawayo

If you are in the Bulawayo area don't forget to visit the Natural History Museum, which houses the largest ornithological collection in the southern hemisphere.

The Zambezi Valley

Lake Kariba and the parks and reserves to the east are very rewarding in January and December. However, Mana Pools is closed at this time.

Mana Pools has six main habitats where 377 species of birds have been observed.

The relatively new ecosystem created by Lake Kariba has attracted many fish eagles and other water birds such as herons, cormorants and the rare Pel's fishing owl. Peregrine falcons also occur here. All these birds are under the threat of extinction as the shells of their eggs are being weakened by the presence of the insecticide DDT in the parents' diet. DDT is not yet banned in Zimbabwe and is used as a crop spray and for the control of malaria and tsetse flies. It is worth noting that an unusual but extremely worthwhile way of birdwatching along the Zambezi River is by canoe. Consult page 66 for information on canoe safaris.

Books that you might wish to consult include *Newman's Birds of Southern Africa*, by Kenneth Newman, published by Southern Books 1992, *Irwin's Birds of Zimbabwe*, by Michael P. Stuart Irwin, published by Quest, Harare 1981. *Bundu Guide Series*, Peter Steyn's book on the 413 species of birds at Hwange, is also invaluable, as is *Top Birding Spots in Southern Africa*, by Hugh Chittenden, published by Southern Books, 1992.

The Ornithological Association of Zimbabwe was, at the time of writing, about to go to press with a book on where to watch birds in Zimbabwe. Contact them at P. O. Box 8382 Causeway, Harare.

CRAFT AND SOUVENIR HUNTING

There is a large range of crafts and souvenirs to choose from throughout Zimbabwe. However, compared with some other African countries, little can be purchased off the street. It must be stressed that what is available on the road in one part of the country is seldom available in another part. So avid buyers of curios should be wary of putting off the purchase of a particular item in the hope of getting a better price or quality elsewhere.

As in many other African countries, crafts are fashioned out of available resources and in Zimbabwe the main products are wood, pottery, sculpted stone, verdite, basketry, woven mats, copperwork, leatherware and woven fabrics.

In certain areas which are well frequented by tourists, such as Victoria Falls, it is difficult to bargain with street or stall sellers, who have a pretty firm idea of what the majority of tourists are prepared to pay. However, in the most remote areas you may be able to knock a couple of dollars off the first price asked.

Where to go

This section lists a number of curio shops and outlets that stock goods likely to appeal to the souvenir hunter.

Harare and environs

Calabash Crafts, 101 Robert Mugabe Road.

Chapungu Gallery Shona Sculpture, Doon Estate, No. 1, Harrow Road, Beverly East, Msasa, Harare. Sculpture gallery and garden.

Chikomo Gallery and Crescent Gems, 2 Skipper Hoste Drive, Kopje, Harare. Shona stone and wood carvings, pottery, basketry, leatherware, embroidery and gemstones, mat weaving.

Cold Comfort Farm Trust, open 07:00 to 17:00, Monday to Saturday, Tel (14) 70-3372. The Trust is 13 km south of Harare on the Bulawayo Road. The co-ops' best products are locally made, designed and dyed tapestries.

Dendera Gallery, Shop No. 4, Arches Houses, corner Second Street and Robert Mugabe Road, Harare. The gallery sells traditional musical instruments, textiles, jewellery, pottery and sculpture and pieces from all over Africa.

Lapidary and African Curio Centre, Linquenda Arcade, 58 Baker Avenue.

The Little Cave, 103 Kaguvi St/Jason Moyale St, for carvings, pottery, t-shirts, stone sculptures, tie-dye textiles, Java print and Tonga handcrafts from the Binga area.

Matombo Gallery, 6 Zimre Centre, 114 Leopold Takawira St (formerly Moffat St), Tel (14) 79-2472. The gallery sells stone sculpture and ethnic paintings, also exhibits widely overseas.

Mbare Market, Chamunika Street, Harare. Here you take pot luck and most of the pleasure comes from browsing around and finding bargains.

Mabwe Gallery, 129 Union Avenue, Harare City Centre. This small exclusive gallery specialises in contemporary African art.

Malwatte Art and Craft Gallery, some 82 km from Harare on the Mutare Road, Tel (179) 3239.

National Gallery Shop, Park Lane/Julius Nyerere Way, open daily 09:00 to 17:00. Stocks sculptures and a wide variety of other crafts, including musical instruments, clothing, basketry.

The National Handicraft Centre, corner Grant and Chinhoyi Streets, open Monday to Saturday 09:30 to 17:00, Tel (14) 72–1816. The centre sells basketry, pottery, mats, weaving, stone carvings, copperwork and leatherware.

Sandros Gallery, Kine Centre, Julius Nyerere Way, Harare. Sells and exhibits stone sculpture.

Sculptors' World, 30 Wonder Shopping Centre, Julius Nyerere Way, Tel (14) 72–0507.

Solo Arts and Crafts, The Parkade, Samora Machel Avenue, Harare. Stone and wooden carvings, gameskin products, copperware, enamelware and leather goods.

Space Age Products, 54 Edison Crescent, Graniteside, Harare, Tel (14) 72–2349. The company sells gameskin products, jewellery, semi-precious stones, copper and brassware.

Stone Dynamics Sculpture Gallery, 56 Samora Machel Avenue, Harare, open Monday to Friday 08:00 to 17:00, Saturday 08:30 to 13:h00. Tel (14) 70–2508.

Vukutu Gallery Sculpture Garden, 9 Harvey Brown Avenue, corner Blakiston Street, Milton Park, Harare. Open daily 09:00 to 18:00, Tel (14) 72–0767. Features over 900 works of art representing 50 sculptors.

Zimba Craft Co-operative, 5 The Parkade, Samora Machel Avenue, Harare, Tel (14) 70–7201. Features interesting clothes and fabrics, basketware, pottery and beadwork.

Bulawayo

Jairos Jiri Craft Shop, Robert Mugabe Way, city centre. This welfare shop was founded to assist disabled and blind people throughout Zimbabwe. The shop in Bulawayo is the biggest in Zimbabwe and features batik, macrame, lampshades, pottery, wall hangings, leather handbags, crocheted tablecloths (Zimbabweans are especially skilled in crochet work) and bedspreads, beadwork and basketry, sisal matting, wooden walking sticks and carvings and soapstone carvings.

Mzilikazi Arts and Crafts Centre, Taylor Avenue, Mzilikazi. The centre is open from 08:30 to 12:30 and 14:00 to 16:00 on weekdays, Tel (19) 6–7245. Mzilikazi is a non profit-making workshop which sustains a welfare programme. Pottery and art feature strongly and are supported by a school section. The centre has been established for more than 20 years. Stone, wood and ceramic products feature strongly. Note that Mzilikazi products are available elsewhere in Bulawayo and Harare.

Victoria Falls

Mawema Creations, Adam Stander Drive, behind the post office, P. O. Box 139 Victoria Falls, Tel (113) 4334. Sells verdite, soapstone, hardwood and ethnic curios.

Mkhishi Curios, Shop 6 Sopers Centre, P. O. Box 186, Victoria Falls, Tel (113) 4412.

Sopers Curios, Adam Stander Road, sells items in ivory, wood, leather, copper, elephant hide.

Victoria Falls Craft Village, behind the post office, offers a wide range of curios and souvenirs.

Zambezi Art Gallery, corner Fox/Parkway Roads, specialists in ivory, malachite, soapstone and wooden curios.

Zambezi Trading, Shop No 4, Victoria Falls Centre, Tel (113) 4426. Sells ethnic jewellery, fabrics, basketware, pottery, carvings, beadwork and clay items.

Hotels: Most of the hotels in Victoria Falls have their own private curio shops to which visitors are most welcome. These sell a wide selection of curios, often together with a range of safari-type clothing.

Nyanga region

Dilly Crafts, P. O. Box 86 Nyanga, Tel (129–8) 222 or 336, features a good selection of local crafts, basketware and woven rugs.

Nyamhuka Craft Centre in Nyamhuka township.

Troutbeck Inn, Montclair Casino Hotel and Brondesbury Park Hotel.

Zuwa Weaving co-op situated in the centre of Nyanga town, has woollen and cotton rugs and blankets, hand-dyed with natural dyes.

Lake Kariba

Hotels: Most of the hotels have their own curio shops in which they sell a variety of craft items. In this area the Batonga tribe's influence and individuality are evident in the carvings, beadwork and winnowing baskets.

Roadside stalls

Masvingo/Beitbridge road

Along this road are many roadside stalls selling pottery, wood carvings, beads and soapstone items. The stall holders are particularly keen to barter their wares for clothes, batteries, radios and pencils, plus a bit of cash.

Masvingo/Chimanimani road

About 11 km after passing over Birchenough Bridge and heading east, you'll come across a fairly substantial collection of craft stalls featuring a wide range of basketry whose style is individual to this part of the country. It is worth stopping here for there are no other craft stalls on the main roads in the region.

Masvingo/Great Zimbabwe

Near the entrance to the Great Zimbabwe Hotel there is a fairly large group of curio sellers. The shape of the Zimbabwe bird features strongly in wood and stone carvings. Also available are bows and real steel tipped arrows, drums, pottery guineafowl and pottery bowls decorated in the distinctive style of the region.

Kariba

Apart from the Nyaminyami (river god/snake) walking stick carvings the most commonly available craft item in this area is crochetwork. Superbly crafted single and double bedspreads, tablecloths and all kinds of mats and doilies are for sale here at very reasonable prices, considering the amount of work that goes into them. Try in particular the viewpoint from Kariba Heights.

Victoria Falls

Outside Victoria Falls, on the airport road, are a number of craft areas especially set aside for sellers. Fat wooden hippo and rhino carvings with much larger but more elegant giraffe carvings are widely available, as well as various types of interesting musical instruments.

ANGLING

With over 7 000 man-made dams, including the "big daddy" of them all, Lake Kariba, and some 90 established angling clubs, fishing in Zimbabwe is a well developed pastime.

Of the more than 117 species found in the country's waters, the tiger fish is perhaps the most renowned. Its razor-like teeth add enormously to its reputation as the best fighting "game" fish for its size in the world. The average tiger fish caught in Kariba weighs 3 kg.

If you wish to plan a fishing holiday, or want to update yourself on the latest fishing "hotspots" or fishing competitions, it's best to make contact with the National Anglers Union of Zimbabwe, P. O. Box ST 950, Southerton, Harare.

Most types of tackle can be purchased at the main shopping areas and sometimes resorts hire out gear. Should you need any particularly sophisticated equipment, it is best to bring your own.

Fishing licences and permits are not always required, but when they are, they may be bought in Bulawayo and in Harare as well as at the various National Parks offices where fishing facilities are available.

It is worth noting that bilharzia is present in the majority of watercourses in Zimbabwe, except perhaps for the cold, fast-flowing mountain streams in the Eastern Highlands.

Where to go for what kind of fish

Barbel, black bass, bottle-nose and bream, carp, cornish jack, mudsucker and pink lady are just a few of the types of freshwater fish waiting for the keen angler to come and try his luck.

The International Tigerfishing Contest is held in October every year in the narrow, 12 km long Sanyati Gorge in Matusadona National Park, south of Kariba and bordering on Lake Kariba. This is the largest freshwater fishing competition in the world and teams from many countries come back year after year, not only for the excellent fishing opportunities but also for the unsurpassed surroundings.

There are also excellent fishing camps in the Binga area, between Deka and Sengwa.

Tiger fish can also be had above the Victoria Falls, upstream of the town, along Zambezi River Drive, where sites have been laid out on the pleasant and shady banks of the river within the Zambezi National Park. There are a number of fishing camps in this area including Kandahar (open all year), Sansimba and Mpala Jena (open from 1 May to 31 October).

There is no agreed method for catching tiger fish and different theories regarding tackle and bait abound. While in Kariba you can purchase bait from Blue Water Charters, Tel (161) 2971/2 or Winsor Diesels, Tel (161) 2864. Fresh kapenta is sold by Irvin and Johnson while most marinas can provide bait to their customers.

If you land a big one and fancy having it on your wall, contact Andora Distributors, Tel (161) 2480, for taxidermy services. Remember to keep the fish damp or it will not be possible to mount it.

Trout fishing

The trout fishing season is from 1 October to 31 May in the dams and streams of the Eastern Highlands, with the exception of Nyanga and Nyangwe dams, which can be fished all year round. The best trout fishing is between January and April.

All conditions and regulations of fishing can be examined at the warden's office in Nyanga National Park and permits may be purchased for the following waters: Rhodes, Mare, Purdon and Udu dams, Nyangombe, Gaerisi, Marora and Pungwe rivers and Lake Gulliver and Saunyami Dam. Nyangwe Dam also features trout hatcheries and research stations. Remember to bring your own rod. Apart from the public dams mentioned, there are private dams and streams in the Nyanga area which also harbour trout. Fishing is permitted on payment of a fee. These private waters include Montclair Casino Hotel and Troutbeck Inn, Lake Alexander, 37 km north of Mutare (near Penhalonga), and Chimanimani National Park.

Zimbabwe has three types of trout: the rarer but more easily caught brown trout, of which the largest caught in Nyanga was just over 3 kg, the even scarcer American brook trout and the common but rewarding rainbow trout. The record for rainbow trout caught in the Nyanga district is 3,827 kg.

FOR SAFARI ENTHUSIASTS

In recent years the safari business has boomed and in the process become diversified, catering to a wide variety of tourist tastes. Today visitors can choose from rail safaris, buffalo safaris, balloon safaris, horseback and foot safaris and even photographic safaris.

Most of the companies running safaris in Zimbabwe offer an exclusive experience with comfortable accommodation and very well trained guides. Of course all this personalised attention costs money – but the memories you are likely to take back home with you are often well worth the expense.

Sailing safaris

Kariba Yacht Safaris offers highly recommended, self-sail cruise packages on 22-ft yachts that accommodate two adults and two children or maybe three adults. You do your own sailing in the company of a "mother ship" and four or five other yachts. You don't need to be experienced as you will be given advance guidance and full instructions. Packages last from two to 14 or more days, depending on demand. While sailing, you can indulge other passions such as photography, fishing, game viewing, birdwatching, swimming and sunbathing, or just relaxing, drinking beer and eating biltong.

The sailing season on Lake Kariba lasts from April to September only and bookings are taken from November to March. Contact Harare Tel (14) 73–6789 or 79–0277 or Cutty Sark Marina, P. O. Box 80 Kariba. Contact Safari Interlink for details of other sailing safaris, Tel Harare (14) 72-0527.

Ox-wagon safaris

Offered on farms in the Highveld region of Zimbabwe in ox-wagons of pioneer origin which seat up to ten people. The safaris last one and a half days or more. Contact Miltana Safaris, P.O. Box 229 Kwekwe, Tel (155) 24-7712.

Balloon safaris

The hot air balloon has finally made it to Victoria Falls and offers a lengthier and more peaceful alternative to the 15-minute "Flight of Angels" over the falls. Contact United Touring Company, Tel Victoria Falls (113) 4267/8 at Zimbank Building, Livingstone Way, Victoria Falls or in Harare Tel (14) 72–7571.

Rail safaris

For those who are hooked on old steam locomotives, the best option is to take a champagne steam safari. The trip takes five days and traverses prime game country.

Alternatively a 12-hour overnight trip gets you by steam locomotive from Bulawayo to Victoria Falls, leaving daily at 17:30. The trip each way affords opportunities for viewing game at dawn and dusk as the track runs through country that abounds in game. Meals are available in the dining car and a bedding ticket must be purchased before boarding the train, preferably when you purchase your ticket. Contact Rail Safaris, Chancellor House, Samora Machel Avenue, P. O. Box 4070, Harare, Tel (14) 73-6056.

Photographic safaris

A number of safari operators (see list on page 79) offer photographic safaris lasting up to 12 days by foot, vehicle, on horseback or canoe. Most operators do their best to ensure your maximum comfort.

Horseback safaris

Horse riding is possible in a number of national parks; it is a superb way of seeing the countryside and getting far closer to the game than you would in a vehicle. If you can't ride but are still keen, remember that you will be exceedingly stiff and sore after the first day or two of riding. Most outrides in the national parks are accompanied by guides and, depending on who is offering them, they can last from an hour and a half to a few days.

Rides are also available at Lake Chivero (formerly Lake Kyle), Troutbeck, Montclair and Brondesbury Park hotels in Juliasdale, near Nyanga and Nyanga National Park.

Hunting safaris

Differentiated into lowveld and highveld hunting, hunting safaris are most usually offered on huge game ranches of thousands of acres, some of which have "big five" game. Hunting is generally used as a way to cull surplus populations of wildlife. In many cases part of the income received from culling is channelled into wildlife conservation programmes.

Bulawayo is well situated to offer access to both lowveld and highveld hunting.

The Wildlife Producers Co-op

This group, comprising some 70 members, has been established to open up lodges and camps on farms and ranches to tourists. Facilities offered include campsites, tented camps, permanent bush camps, luxury lodges and farm home-stays. Prices also vary widely but the Co-op has endeavoured to establish a certain standard. Full board and self-catering options are available and the emphasis is on small select groups and farm hosts try to make them feel more like guests than tourists.

Members include farmers of tobacco, pedigree cattle, maize, soya beans and cotton, dairy and livestock.

The following list is not exhaustive. New companies may have formed and others ceased trading since the time of writing. For more details contact Wildlife Producers Co-operative, P. O. Box 592, Harare, Tel (14) 30-4993/70-3978, or visit their office in George Silundika Avenue, between First and Angwa Streets.

Establishment	Address	Telephone	Operating area
Abercrombie & Kent	P. O. Box 2997 Harare	Harare (14) 72-5511 Kariba (161) 2321	
African Antelope Safaris	P. O. Box 42 Mvuma	Mvuma (132) 2106	Highveld Plains game
African Escapes	P. O. Box 3065 Harare	Harare (14) 3-9633	Photographic safaris
Alko Ranching	P. O. Box 9 Mwenezi	Mwenezi (114-7) 3703	Ranch hunting
Assegai Safaris	P. O. Box 348 Kadoma	Kadoma (168) 3222	Ranch hunting
Astra Wildlife	P. O. Box 55 Kariba	Kariba (161) 2-2512	Big game
Backpackers Africa	P. O. Box 125 Victoria Falls		
Baird Ranch Safaris	P. O. Box 572 Kwekwe	Munyati (155-7) 2425	Highveld ranch hunting
Bangala Ranch	8 Lamorby Close Highlands Harare	Harare (14) 4-5429	Ranch hunting
Bar G Ranching & Safaris	7 Whitman Road Bulawayo	Bulawayo (19) 4-2952	Ranch hunting and plains game
Binga Wildlife Safaris	P. O. Box 129 Chiredzi	Chiredzi (131) 2786	Ranch hunting

80 Zimbabwe

Establishment	Address	Telephone	Operating area
Black Rhino Safaris	P. O. Box FM89 Famona Bulawayo	Bulawayo (19) 4-1662	Photographic and water safaris
Bon Voyage Travel	P. O. Box 2193 Bulawayo	Bulawayo (19) 7-4061	Travel agency
Bubi Safaris	P. O. Box 29 Chiredzi	Chiredzi (131) 5-2924	Lowveld plains game
Budget Tours	P. O. Box UA 282 Harare	Harare (14) 79-0360	Travel agency
Buffalo Range Safaris	P.O. Buffalo Range Triangle	Triangle (133) 362	Zambezi catchment big/plains game
Buffalo Safaris	P. O. Box 113 Kariba	Kariba (161) 2827	Zambezi catchment Photographic and hunting
Call of Africa	P. O. Box 371 Karoi	Karoi (164) 4-1296	
Carolina Wilderness	P. O. Box W83 Waterfalls	Harare (14) 2-9565	
Chikwenya Safaris	P/Bag 2081 Kariba	Kariba (161) 2253	
Centrust Travel	P. O. Box 1593 Harare	Harare (14) 70-4313	
Chimanimani Africa Tours	P. O. Box 4479 Harare	Harare (14) 6-8451	
Chimwara Ranch Company	P. O. Box 180 Bulawayo	Bulawayo (19) 4-2626	Ranch hunting
Chinyika Ranch Safaris	P. O. Box 232 Kwekwe	Kwekwe (155) 24-7520	Ranch hunting
Chipimbi Safaris	P. O. Box 29 Chiredzi	Chiredzi (131) 5-2924	Lowveld plains game
Chipimbere Safaris	P. O. Box 9 Kariba	Kariba (161) 2839	Photographic canoeing safaris
Chipoli Safaris	P. O. Box 1800 Shamva	Shamva 303	
Chiredzi Safaris	P. O. Box 10 Triangle	Triangle (131) 2913	Lowveld
Chiredzi Wildlife Investment Company (Pvt) Ltd	P. O. Box 241 Chiredzi Harare	Chiredzi (131) 2913 (14) 2-4022	Big game

What to do 81

Establishment	Address	Telephone	Operating area
Chris Worden Safaris	P. O. Box 221 Kariba	Kariba (161) 2433	Backpacking
Connolly Safaris	P. O. Box 762 Bulawayo	Bulawayo (19) 6–3202	Lowveld ranch hunting
Darcal Wildlife Safaris	P. O. Box 22 W. Nicholson	(116) 5202	Plains game
Denda Safaris	P. O. Box 20 Philips Avenue Belgravia Harare	Harare (14) 72–7197	Big game
Denlar Safaris	P. O. Box 52 Victoria Falls	Victoria Falls (113) 4335	Zambezi catchment Big/plains game
Deonsteffen Safaris	P. O. Box 22 Gwaai	Gwaai 2104	Big game
Dombawara Game Trails	P. O. Box 205 Bindura		Photographic safaris
Doorn Hoek Ranch	P. O. Box 227 Karoi	Karoi (164) 2–9125	Highveld ranch hunting
Dziva	P. O. Box 1 Kariba	Kariba (161) 2697	
Eden Safaris	P. O. Box 232 Chinhoyi	Chinhoyi (167) 27–9323	Ranch hunting
Edenvale Safaris	P. O. Box 6 Mwenezi		Plains game
Elephant Hills Safaris	P. O. Box 6638 Harare	Harare (14) 24–7619	Plains game
Ferry Tours	P. O. Box UA 176 Harare	Harare (14) 4–2990	
Flip Nicholson Safaris	P. O. Box 1380 Harare	Harare (14) 73–8442	Photographic
Fothergill Island	P. O. Box 2081 Kariba	Kariba (161) 2253	Backpacking, river and game viewing
Fountain Hunting	P. O. Box 20 Nyamandhlovu	(187) 220	Ranch hunting
Gambudi Ranch	P. O. Box 150 Chinhoyi	Chinhoyi (167) 27–9322	Highveld ranch hunting
Gametrackers	P. O. Box 133 Victoria Falls	Victoria Falls (113) 4381	
Garth Thompson Safaris	P. O. Box 5826 Harare	Harare (14) 79–5202	All types of safaris
Gavin Rabinovitch	P. O. Box 216 Hwange	Hwange (181) 5–5521	Zambezi catchment Big/plains game

82 Zimbabwe

Establishment	Address	Telephone	Operating area
Geoff Cox Adventures	P. O. Box A456 Avondale	Harare (14) 3-5692	
Goliath Safaris	P. O. Box CH294 Chisipite	Harare (14) 70-8843	Wilderness trails Canoeing safaris
Guyu Safaris	P. O. Box 179 Victoria Falls	Victoria Falls (113) 42-4513	Big game
Gwaai Valley Safaris	P. O. Box 17 Gwayi	Dete (118) 2304	Big game
HHK Safaris	35 Kirklands Road Greenhills	Bulawayo (19) 3-0663	Plains game
	P. O. Box 22 Triangle	Triangle (133) 6423	Plains game
Hankano Ranch	P. O. Box 17 Gwayi	Dete (118) 0-0321	Gwayi river area ranch hunting
Henderson & Sons	P. O. Box 2217 Bulawayo	Bulawayo (19) 6-8669	Ranching company
Hippo Pools Camp	P. O. Box 90 Shamva	Shamva (171-8) 1123	Safari camp, game viewing
Hippo Valley Safaris	P. O. Box 1 Chiredzi	Chiredzi (131) 381	Zambezi catchment Big/plains game
Horse Safaris	P. O. Box 43 Dete	Dete (118) 255	Horseback safaris
Humani Safaris	P/Bag 7020 Chiredzi	Chiredzi (131) 2623	Ranch hunting
Hunters Safaris	P. O. Mbalabala	Esigodini (188) 25-5529	Lowveld areas Big/plains game
Hunters Track	P. O. Box 4 Chisipite Harare	Arcturus (14) 2-7716	Zambezi catchment Big/plains game
Hwange Safaris	P/Bag 5792 Dete	Hwange (181) 331	
Imire Game Park	P/Bag 3570 Marondera	Wedza (122) 0-5032	
Ingwalati Safaris	P. O. Box 418 Kwe Kwe	Kwe Kwe (155) 3-6892	Ranch hunting
Ingwe Safaris	P. O. Box 1870 Harare	Harare (14) 4-4910	Ranch hunting
Inhlaba Safaris	P. O. Box 1472 Bulawayo	Bulawayo (19) 6-8379	Ranch hunting and plains game

Establishment	Address	Telephone	Operating area
International Cattle Company	P. O. Box 280 Avondale Harare	Munyati (155–7) 2–4022	Highveld ranch hunting
International Tour Centre	P. O. Box 4275 Harare	Harare (14) 79–2575	Travel agent
Into Africa	P. O. Box 2284 Bulawayo	Bulawayo (19) 4–1725	Plains game
Ivory Safaris	P. O. Box 9127 Hillside Bulawayo	Bulawayo (19) 6–1709	Photographic safaris
Iwaba Safaris	P. O. Box 5 Kwekwe	Kwekwe (155) 24–7723	Big game safaris
Jed Robinson	P. O. Box 145 Victoria Falls	Victoria Falls (113) 4486	Backpacking, canoeing safaris
Jet Tours	P. O. Box 3622 Harare	Harare (14) 79–3081	Travel agent
Kalambeza Safaris	P. O. Box 121 Victoria Falls	Victoria Falls (113) 4480	Backpacking, boating safaris
Kariba cruises	P. O. Box A88 Harare		
Kariba Yacht	6 Fairfield Road Hatfield Harare	Harare (14) 5–0305	Sailing safaris
Kazungula Wildlife	P. O. Box 132 Victoria Falls	Victoria Falls (113) 43–0521	Zambezi catchment
Kavisa Safaris	P. O. Box 220 Kwekwe	Kwekwe (155) 2475–22	Plains game
Kelvin Hills Safari	P. O. Box 139 Kadoma	Munyati (155–7)	Highveld ranch hunting
Kudu Safaris	P. O. Box 29 Turk Mine	Turk Mine (185) 0–1912	Ranch hunting
Kuvhima Safaris	7 Cinnamon Close Chisipite	Harare (14) 4–4839	Ranch hunting
Lake Safaris	P. O. Box 34 Kariba	Kariba (161) 2752	
Landela Safaris	P. O. Box 66293 Harare	Harare (14) 70–2634	All types of safari
Lennox Kruger	P. O. Box FM 264 Famona	Bulawayo (19) 7–7540	Ranch hunting

84 Zimbabwe

Establishment	Address	Telephone	Operating area
Leopard Ridge Hunting Company	P. O. Box 1348 Bulawayo	Bulawayo (19) 4-9266	Ranch hunting
Lions Den Safaris	P. O. Box 19 Gwayi	Dete (118) 0-0112	Zambezi catchment (Mainly) plains game
Lone Star Safaris	P/Bag 7004 Chiredzi	Chiredzi (131) 3-6919	Zambezi catchment Big/plains game
Lowveld Hunters	P. O. Box 36 Triangle	Triangle (133) 62-7917	
Lowveld Safaris	P. O. Box 8408 Harare	Harare (14) 70-9068	Lowveld ranch hunting
Madoda Ranch Safaris	P. O. Box 286 Kadoma	Kadoma (168) 3-1363	Plains game
Mana Pools	P/Bag 2081 Kariba	Kariba (161) 2253	
Manica Travel Services	P. O. Box 3141 Harare	Harare (14) 70-3421 Bulawayo (19) 6-2521	Travel agency
Mashura Ranch	P. O. Box 14 W. Nicholson	(116) 4201	Ranch hunting
Matabele Hunters	P. O. Box 4 Nyamandhlovu	(187) 2-3629	
Matetsi Safaris	P. O. Box 160 Victoria Falls	Victoria Falls (113) 4557	Zambezi catchment Big/plains game
Mitchell Cotts Travel	P. O. Box 1883 Bulawayo	Bulawayo (19) 6-8631	Travel agency
Mokambi Wildlife	P. O. Box 129 Chiredzi	Chiredzi (131) 2876	
Mkwasini Game Ranch	P. O. Box 113 Chiredzi	Chiredzi (131) 5-5917	Lowveld ranch hunting
Msena Ranch Safaris	P. O. Box A100 Avondale	Harare (14) 3-9275	Plains game
Mungwezi Ranch	P. O. Box 297 Chiredzi	Chiredzi (131) 2640	Walking safaris, plains game safaris
Munyati Ranch	P. O. Box 520 Kwekwe	Kwekwe (155) 24-7525	Ranch hunting
Musanga Safaris	P. O. Box 8024 Belmont	Harare (14) 70-3729	Lowveld plains game
Muvimi Safaris	P. O. Box 2233 Harare	Harare (14) 3-4933	Ranch safaris
Miltana Safaris	P. O. Box 229 Kwekwe	Kwekwe (155) 2092	

What to do

Establishment	Address	Telephone	Operating area
Mwari Komborera	P. O. Box 130 Victoria Falls		
Mziki Safaris	P. O. Box 12 Nyamandhlovu	(187) 2–3624	Ranch hunting
National Safaris	P. O. Box UA 191 Union Ave	Harare (14) 73–0771	Zambezi catchment big/plains game
Ngamo Safaris	P. O. Box 467 Bulawayo	Bulawayo (19) 6–1495	Zambezi catchment big/plains game
Nkwazi Safaris	P. O. Box 45 Victoria	Victoria Falls (113) 4326	Zambezi catchment big game
Norzim Bushtrek	P/Bag 7520 Chinhoyi	Chinhoyi (167) 26–9321	
Nuanetsi Hunters	P. O. Box 22 Chiredzi	Chiredzi (127) 575	Lowveld Mainly plains game
	P. O. Box 2006 Mwenezi	Mwenezi (114–7) 6	Plains game
Nyayasha Ranch	P. O. Box 177 Chiredzi	Chiredzi (131) 2557	Plains game safaris
Nyedzi nyedzi	P. O. Box 15 W. Nicholson	(116) 5605	Ranch hunting
Orion Hunters	P. O. Box 444 Chinhoyi	Chinhoyi (167) 26–9523	Ranch hunting
P.D. Seymore-Smith	P. O. Box 5 Kwekwe	Kwekwe (155) 24–7723	Zambezi catchment big/plains game
PM's Safaris	P. O. Box A 583 Avondale	Harare (14) 30–2233	Ranch hunting
Paul Grobler Safaris	P. O. Box 391 Marondera	Marondera (179) 34–2220	Zambezi catchment big/plains game
Peter Garvin	P. O. Box UA 93 Union Avenue	Harare (14) 30–2781	Canoeing and walking
Phileas Fogg Travel	P. O. Box 5454 Harare	Harare (14) 70–4141	Travel agency
Rail Safaris	P. O. Box 4070 Harare	Harare (14) 73–6056	Steam train safaris
Ranch Safaris	P. O. Box 202 Bulawayo	Bulawayo (19) 6–5081	Gwaai plains game
Roselyn Safaris	P/Bag 5934 Hwange	Hwange (181) 7–0223	Zambezi catchment big/plains game
Ross Travel	P. O. Box 5405 Harare	Harare (14) 79–5386	Travel agency

86 Zimbabwe

Establishment	Address	Telephone	Operating area
Rosslyn Safaris	P. O. Box 5934 Hwange	Hwange (181) 7-0223	Big game
Royal Travel	P. O. Box 1166 Bulawayo	Bulawayo (19) 6-9521	Travel agency
Ruwanzi Ranch	P. O. Box 452 Karoi	Karoi (164) 63-5216	Plains game
Sable Home Safaris	P. O. Box 130 Kadoma	Kadoma (168) 3-1413	Ranch hunting
Sable Safaris	P. O. Box 153 Mhangura	Mhangura (160) 5-7916 (160) 5-5247	Ranch hunting
Safari Consultants	P. O. Box 5826 Harare	Harare (14) 79-5202	
Safari Interlink	P. O. Box 5920 Harare	Harare (14) 72-0527	All types of safari
Safari Operators	P. O. Box UA 191 Harare	Harare (14) 73-0771	Operators' association
Safari Par Excellence	P. O. Box CH 69	Harare (14) 73-0771	
Safari Services	P. O. Box 3 Kariba	Kariba (161) 2433	
Safari Trackers	1 Hoopoe Hollow Burnside	Bulawayo (19) 4-3207	Plains game
Safari Travel Agency	P. O. Box 185 Victoria Falls	Victoria Falls (113) 4571	
Sanyati Safaris	P. O. Box 2008 Kariba	Harare (14) 79-5655	Lodges and river safaris
Savanna Wildlife	P. O. Box 1830 Harare	Harare (14) 70-6661	Plains game
Sarbo Safaris	P. O. Box 22 Chiredzi		Lowveld
Savannah Safaris	P. O. Box 166 Beitbridge	Beitbridge (186) 302	Plains game
Sebakwe Safaris	P. O. Box 44 Kwekwe	Kwekwe (155) 24-7825	Highveld ranch hunting
Sentinel Limpopo Services	P. O. Box 36 Beitbridge	Beitbridge (186) 4-3521	Lowveld plains game
Shearwater Adventure	P. O. Box 3961 Harare	Harare (14) 73-5712	River safaris, ballooning
S.K. Cawood	P/Bag 5730 Beitbridge	Mwenezi (114-7) 0-1340	Lowveld ranch hunting

What to do

Establishment	Address	Telephone	Operating area
Spurwing Island	P. O. Box 101 Kariba	Kariba (161) 2466	
Sunrise Safaris	P. O. Box 485 Bulawayo	Bulawayo (19) 6–7551	Fishing safaris
Sunshine Tours	P. O. Box 447 Bulawayo	Bulawayo (19) 6–7791	
Thunghata Safaris Group	P. O. Box 1348 Bulawayo	Bulawayo (19) 4–3109	Ranch hunting
Tshabezi Safaris	P. O. Box 35 W. Nicholson	(116) 318	Ranch hunting
Touch the Wild Safaris	P/Bag 5779 Dete	Dete (118) 2105	
Track-a-hunt Safaris	P. O. Box 91 Banket	Banket (166) 3212	Ranch hunting
Trackers Safaris	P. O. Box EH 9 Emerald Hill	Harare (14) 3–9886	Game viewing
Travel Tourist Safaris	P. O. Box HG 470 Harare	Harare (14) 4–4990	Big game
Trophy Hunters	P. O. Box 147 Victoria Falls	Victoria Falls (113) 43–3519	Zambezi catchment Big/plains game
Twin Spring Ranch	P. O. Box 23 Kwekwe	Kwekwe (155) 24–7512	Ranch hunting
UTC	P. O. Box 2914 Harare	Harare (14) 79–3071 Kariba (161) 2662	All types of safaris
Umfurudzi Bush Camps	P. O. Box 90 Shamva	Shamva (171–8) 31/51	
Vadoma Safaris	P. O. Box 154 Kwekwe	Kwekwe (155) 3–8764	Zambezi catchment Big/plains game
Van der Riet Safaris	P. O. Box UA 191 Union Ave Harare	Harare (14) 73–0771	Big game
Victoria Falls Hunters	P. O. Box 1 Mufakose Harare	Harare (14) 6–8311	Big game
Welcombe Travel	P. O. Box 166 Harare	Harare (14) 70–8067	
Western Safaris	P. O. Box 8488 Bulawayo	Bulawayo (19) 7–6111	Big/plains game Zambezi catchment

88 Zimbabwe

Establishment	Address	Telephone	Operating area
Westwood Game Lodge	P. O. Box 132 Victoria Falls	Victoria Falls (113) 4614	
Westwood Wildlife	P. O. Box 21 Victoria Falls	Victoria Falls (113) 4469	Zambezi catchment Big/plains game
Wild Africa Safaris	P. O. Box 2937 Harare	Harare (14) 6-8666	Mavuradona booking agent
Woodlands Safaris	P/Bag 5916 Victoria Falls	Victoria Falls (113) 42-6513	Zambezi catchment Big/plains game
Zambezi Hippo Trails	P. O. Box 47 Mhangura		Lake Kariba and river safaris
Zambezi Horse Trails	P. O. Box 3961 Harare	Harare (14) 73-5712	
Zambezi Hunters	P. O. Box 139 Ruwa	Ruwa (173) 2567	Big/plains game Zimbabwe catchment
Zambezi Safaris	P. O. Box 2554 Harare	Harare (14) 70-3094	Big game Game viewing, fishing
	P. O. Box 159 Victoria Falls	Victoria Falls (113) 4219	
Zambezi Spectacular	P/Bag 2016 Kariba	Kariba (161) 72-8763	Luxury river safari
Zambezi Trails		Harare (14) 73-3719	All types of safari
Zambezi White Water		Harare (14) 70-2364	Zambezi River kayak safaris
Zambezi Wilderness Safaris	P. O. Box 18 Victoria Falls		
Zimbots Photographic	P. O. Box 9022 Centenary	Centenary (157) 2440	Photographic safari
Zimbabwe Safaris	P. O. Box 18 Ruwa	Harare (14) 26-83017	Big/plains game
Zim Ranch Safaris	P. O. Box 238 Kadoma	Kadoma (168) 3-1414	Ranch hunting
Zimtours	P. O. Box 8052 Causeway Harare	Harare (14) 79-3666	Travel agency
Zindele Safaris	P. O. Box 232A Harare	Harare (14) 72-1696	Ranch hunting

OTHER SPORTS

Participatory sports

Swimming

During the hot summer months there's nothing nicer than finding a sparkling blue swimming pool and submerging yourself in it. Many Zimbabwean towns have Olympic-sized public swimming pools while almost all the larger hotels have their own private swimming pools.

If you are staying in a hotel which doesn't have a swimming pool, ask reception staff for the address of the nearest public swimming pool. They are usually clean and very well maintained. Don't bathe in rivers, lakes or dams as you run the risk of catching bilharzia or being attacked by a crocodile. Many Zimbabweans try and combat bilharzia by regularly dosing themselves with a bilharzia treatment. However, this practice is questionable in the long term. Mountain streams and pools in the Eastern Highlands are safer bets as far as bilharzia is concerned.

Tennis

There are tennis courts in most towns, usually run by private clubs. Again, ask your hosts for advice regarding the nearest tennis court.

Fishing

See section on Angling, page 75.

Cycling

See page 106.

Squash

Most clubs have squash courts and several hotels have private squash courts as well.

Gambling

Zimbabwe's four licensed casinos are situated at Kariba, Nyanga and Victoria Falls, all suitably scenic places in which to lose or make a fortune. In Victoria Falls there are two casinos; one in the Makasa Sun, and the other in the recently re-opened Elephant Hills Hotel. In Kariba, the casino is in the Caribbea Bay Hotel complex and in the Eastern Highlands at the Montclair Casino Resort to the west of Nyanga. A new casino was to have been included in the recently rebuilt Leopard Rock Hotel in the Vumba Mountains, outside Mutare.

All the regular casino games are played in these casinos although chips can only be exchanged for foreign currency if you hold a non-Zimbabwean passport.

Golf

Zimbabwe is certainly a golfer's paradise. Most towns have at least one golf course, and there are over 70 in the country as a whole. Harare alone has 16 courses (of 18 holes each), half of which are championship rated.

Apart from being spoilt for choice, the golfer will usually benefit from fine weather and reasonable course rates which include the added bonus of a caddie. Although many clubs offer clubs for hire, bring your own set if you intend to play a lot of golf.

Some of the courses are listed below, together with their lengths.

Harare
Royal Harare 6 467 m, 5th Street Extension, Tel (14) 70–2929, listed in the top 50 outside the United States. It has good restaurant and catering facilities.
Chapman Golf Club 6 524 m, Samora Machel Avenue, Eastlea, Tel (14) 73–6940/73–6949, tighter and more demanding than the Royal Harare.
Country Club 6 143 m, Glenara Avenue, supposedly has crocodiles in its water hazards.
Police Golf Club Josiah Chinamano Avenue, Harare, Tel (14) 72–5232. An open course interspersed with streams.
Warren Hills Golf Club 6 666 m, Tel (14) 79–2323. Old Kadoma Road, 8 km from centre. Somewhat flat and open.
Wingate Park Club 6 384 m, 16 km outside Harare on Alps Road off Borrowdale Road, Tel (14) 88–2224. The course is flattish with pine-fringed fairways.
Harare South Country Club 6 169 m, Tel (14) 6–7584, 23 km along Masvingo Road. A flat course surrounded by the ever-changing msasa trees.
Ruwa Country Club 6 344 m, Tel (275) 2376, 29 km from the centre of Harare. Ruwa is a fairly wooded course and has a pleasant pub at the 19th hole.

Golf Driving Range situated on Samora Machel Avenue, to the east of the Park Lane Hotel (Tel (14) 4–7811). The driving range has a golf shop selling accessories and drinks. There is a putt-putt course next door.

Outside Harare

Bulawayo Country Club 6 186 m, Old Esigodini Road, Tel (19) 4–9677, 10 km from centre of town with championship rating.

Harry Allen Golf Club 6 456 m, Tel (19) 6–3845, 4 km from the centre of Bulawayo.

Bulawayo Golf Club 6 431 m, Tel (19) 6–7067, 3 km from town, undulating, trees, championship rated.

Chinhoyi 6 494 m, Tel (167) 2383. Undulating course.

Enterprise 6 127 m, 34 km from Harare on Shamva Road.

Karoi 6 475 m Tel (164) 6200–11. Two hundred kilometres north of Harare on the Kariba Road.

Marondera 6 190 m, Tel (179) 3591, Ruzawi Road.

Victoria Falls Elephant Hills Country Club, recently reopened for the Commonwealth Conference. A unique course as players have to negotiate crocodiles and warthogs, snakes and even the odd hippo. The course is set on the banks of the Zambezi and the Victoria Falls are just a few kilometres downstream. Originally designed by Gary Player, the Elephant Hills course was much longer before it was closed down after a mortar attack in 1977, although it is still rated as one of the toughest in Africa. Twenty electric golf carts have been brought into service to help golfers beat the heat when walking around this demanding course.

Chegutu Golf Club 6 303 m, Tel (153) 2266, adjacent to Chegutu town.

Eiffel Flats Golf Club 6 376 m, 10 km to the east of Kadoma.

Gweru Golf Club 6 218 m, Tel (154) 3 493, just 1 km outside town, flattish, lots of bunkers, water hazards.

Kadoma Golf Club 6 218 m, Tel (168) 3652, 1 km outside town.

Shurugwi Golf Club 6 083 m, 2 km outside town, a scenic but very demanding course.

Masvingo 6 278 m.

Hippo Valley Country Club Tel (131) 2381/6 or 2712/5, nine holes, the course had lots of rivers before the 1992 drought.

Mutare 5 973 m, Tel (120) 6–1862, championship rated, 2 km outside city.

Hillside 6 207 m, Tel (120) 6–0721, 3 km from centre of Mutare, championship rated.

Leopard Rock 5 486 m, 32 km outside Mutare. Tough, but very scenic.

Troutbeck 2 602 m, picturesque, hilly, rated the highest course in Africa and known as the "Gleneagles of Africa". You can attempt to drive a ball over the lake but this can prove difficult.

Montclair Casino Hotel, 2 865 m, Tel (129) 441, golf course with hotel accommodation and casino.

Brondesbury Park 2 734 m, Tel (1209) 343, undulating, well situated, hotel accommodation.

Chimanimani Golf Course 2 655 m, Melsetter Country Club, Tel (126) 266. The course is 2 km from the village.

Claremont Golf Club 2 865 m, Juliasdale, Tel (129) 469, hotel accommodation, scenic.

Chipinge Country Club 5 650 m, Tel (127) 2350.

Spectator sports

Soccer

This is by far the most popular spectator sport in Zimbabwe with big matches drawing crowds of over 40 000 during the soccer season from February to November. Visitors may watch league games in all the cities and towns. Watch the press for details.

Horse racing

The two major courses, Ascot and Borrowdale, are situated in Bulawayo and Harare respectively. Like soccer, horse racing is very well supported by Zimbabweans. Although meetings are held all year round, the main racing season is between May and July.

Cricket

Cricket is played during summer in Zimbabwe. Most sports and country clubs have their own cricket pitches. The national side has had some success.

Rugby

Rugby is a perennially popular sport in Zimbabwe, though mostly favoured by the white community. It is usually played during winter.

4. HOW TO GET THERE

As Zimbabwe is a landlocked country, the only ways of getting there are by road, air and train.

BY AIR

Harare airport, some 18 km from the capital, is Zimbabwe's international airport. The buildings and services are rather old-fashioned, but there are basics such as a duty-free shop, a post office, restaurant and bar.

A number of major air links are shared with other countries (see below) so Zimbabwe is easy to get to.

An airport bus which links the airport and the Air Zimbabwe air terminal in Harare runs every hour on the hour from 06:00 to 23:00. A nominal fare is charged.

If you don't feel like waiting for the bus, you could use the more expensive taxis that are sometimes available. Both Hertz and Avis car hire firms operate desks in the terminal from 07:00 until the last flight has landed.

Air Zimbabwe flies to the following international destinations (subject to change): Frankfurt, Larnaca (Cyprus), London, Perth, Athens (via Larnaca), Sydney, Durban, Johannesburg, Lusaka, Mauritius, Manzini (Swaziland), Maputo (Mozambique), Gaborone (Botswana), Lilongwe (Malawi), Nairobi, Windhoek (Namibia) and Dar-es-Salaam (Tanzania). For domestic services see Chapter 5, Travelling inside Zimbabwe (page 123).

Other international airlines flying to Zimbabwe or with connections to Zimbabwe are British Airways, Balkan Bulgarian Airways, Ethiopian Airlines, TAP, Kenya Airways, Ghana Airways, Zambia Airways, Air Malawi and South African Airways.

The following airlines have representatives in Harare:

Air Botswana	Tel (14) 70–3132
Air Malawi	Tel (14) 70–6497
Air Mauritius	Tel (14) 73–5738

Balkan Airlines	Tel (14) 72-9213
British Airways	Tel (14) 79-4616
Ghana Airways	Tel (14) 70-3335
KLM	Tel (14) 70-5430
Mozambique Airlines	Tel (14) 70-3338
Royal Swazi	Tel (14) 73-0170
TAP (Air Portugal)	Tel (14) 70-6231
Zambian Airways	Tel (14) 79-3235
Air India	Tel (14) 70-0318
Air Zimbabwe	Tel (14) 73-7011
Swissair	Tel (14) 70-7712
Ethiopian Airlines	Tel (14) 79-5215
Kenya Airways	Tel (14) 79-2181
Lufthansa	Tel (14) 70-7606
Quantas	Tel (14) 70-3494
South African Airways	Tel (14) 73-8922
UTA/Air France	Tel (14) 70-3868

Flight information can be obtained by telephoning (14) 73-7011.

BY ROAD

A twice-weekly bus travels between Harare and Johannesburg and another bus connects Harare with Lusaka in Zambia and Lilongwe in Malawi. Ask your travel agent for departure times and dates.

There are ten entry points in Zimbabwe:

Neighbouring country	Border post	Opening times daily including public holidays
From Botswana	via Plumtree	06:00 to 18:00
	Mpandamatenga	08:00 to 16:00
	Kasungula	08:00 to 16:00
From Zambia	Victoria Falls	06:00 to 18:00
	Kariba	06:00 to 18:00
	Chirundu	06:00 to 18:00
From Mozambique	Mutare	06:00 to 18:00
	Nyamapanda	06:00 to 18:00
From Namibia	Kasungula	06:00 to 18:00
From South Africa	Beitbridge	06:00 to 20:00

(delays likely on or near to public and school holidays)

From Zambia

You can enter Zimbabwe via Maramba (formerly Livingstone) and Victoria Falls, which will bring you into the western sector of the country with your first major stopover being Bulawayo via Hwange. From Lusaka to the Zimbabwe border at Victoria Falls the distance is 473 km. You could also choose to enter Zimbabwe via Kariba or Chirundu, which continues on the main road to Harare. Distance from Lusaka to Chirundu is 155 km. To reach Kariba, you have to branch off some 18 km from the border and follow a fully tarred road for 65 km. The distance from Kariba to Harare is 369 km with a 77-km link up to the main A1, and from Chirundu to Harare is 352 km.

From Mozambique

In the past informal truck convoys travelled from Beira to Harare (via Mutare) along the so-called Beira Corridor but because of the as yet unresolved bush war (at the time of writing) it is recommended that you fly from Mozambique.

From Malawi

To get from Malawi to Zimbabwe you have to traverse a substantial portion of Mozambique. In the past regular convoys would travel this route accompanied by armed soldiers. However an intensification of the bush war in Mozambique during 1991 resulted in the closure of this route. The convoy may resume operation in the future, however. Confirm the current security status of the route by asking around.

The border post on the Zimbabwean side is at Nyamapanda, 245 km to the north-east of Harare.

To reach Zimbabwe from Malawi there is the much longer but safer alternative route via Zambia and Chirundu (see above).

From South Africa

The Beitbridge border post can become congested with delays lasting several hours. If it is hot, remember to anticipate a long delay by stocking your car with cold drinks and other refreshments. Think twice before travelling in the heat at peak periods with babies and young children. The distance between Beitbridge and Harare is 579 km.

Overland operators

The following companies offer cross-Africa expeditions that end in Harare. The trips take a minimum of five months and start in the United Kingdom.

Name	Britain	Australia	United States
Dragoman Ltd	10 Riverside Framlingham Suffolk 1P139AG Tel (0728) 72-4184	Access Travel 58 Pitt St Sydney 2000 Tel (02) 241 1128	
Guerba Expeditions	101 Eden Vale Rd Westbury Wiltshire BA13 3YB Tel (0373) 82-6689		Adventure Center 5540 College Ave Oakland CA 94618 Tel (800) 227-8747
Exodus Overland	9 Weir Road London SW12 OLT Tel (071) 675-5550	Adventure World 37 York St Sydney NSW 2000 Tel (02) 241-1128	Force 10 Expeditions P. O. Box 8548 Wankegan IL 60079 Tel (312) 336-2070
Encounter Overland	267 Old Brompton Rd London SW5 9JA Tel (071) 370-8645	Sundowners Travel Centre, 108 Albion Street Sydney Tel (02) 281-4066	Booking same as for Guerba Expeditions See above

GETTING INTO ZIMBABWE

Immigration requirements

Visitors require a passport which is valid for a minimum of six months, plus an air ticket either to your country of origin or to a destination outside Zimbabwe, or proof of sufficient funds to cover your stay in Zimbabwe and finance your return trip.

Travellers from the European Community, the Commonwealth, Scandinavian countries and the United States of America do not require entry visas while nationals from the countries listed below do require valid visas on entering Zimbabwe. This list was correct at the time of writing, but check with your travel agent for confirmation or contact the Chief Immigration Officer, Private Bag 7717, Causeway, Harare. The processing of visa applications may take some time, so be sure to apply in good time. See page 181 for a list of diplomatic missions abroad where you may obtain your visa application forms.

List of countries whose nationals may require entry visas:

Afghanistan	Kampuchea	Senegal
Albania	North Korea	Somalia
Algeria	South Korea	South Africa
Andorra	Laos	Spain
Angola	Lebanon	Sudan
Bhutan	Libya	Syria
Bulgaria	Mali	Taiwan
Burma	Mozambique	Tibet
Cape Verde Islands	Mongolia	Vietnam
China	Philippines	South Yemen
CIS (formerly USSR)	Poland	North Yemen
Iran	Portugal	Zaire
Iraq	Romania	

Customs duty

You are permitted to bring in any amount in foreign currency in cash, but this must be declared on a foreign exchange currency declaration form (see page 98). You may also bring in Z$200 worth of consumable goods which are not classed as merchandise imported for trade purposes. Included in this allowance are five litres of alcohol per adult (18 years and over), of which not more than two litres may be spirits, as well as an unlimited supply of tobacco. Items are exempt from duty if they are quite obviously intended for your use during your stay. Members of a family travelling together may pool their allowances.

Firearms

Firearms must be declared on entering Zimbabwe. If you are the client of a safari firm it is permissible to hire firearms from the operators. You should ensure that you have sufficient ammunition before arriving.

Before entering a national park you are required by law to declare any firearms or ammunition you may have with you.

Currency regulations

Most major currencies are accepted and changed at the banks. Note also that only Z$100 per person may be exported (at the time of writing). A superficial body search of departing passengers is usually conducted at the airports. Harare airport bank agency is open from 06:30 to 22:00, for foreign currency transactions only.

There is no restriction on the amount of foreign currency you may import into Zimbabwe. You should be handed a currency declaration form on entry and will be required to complete it, stating exactly how much foreign currency is in your possession. The form will be stamped by the authorities who will retain a copy. If such a form is not handed to you, then demand one, because if you leave the country without producing your part of the currency declaration form you may not be permitted to export your foreign currency. Each time you change money the form must be stamped and you should be given an exchange receipt. If you do happen to lose the form then report it to the authorities without delay, otherwise you will not be able to reconvert your local currency into foreign currency on departure.

A thriving black market exists as a result of the strict foreign exchange controls. Be wary of people approaching you with tempting offers and note that the plainclothes policemen are rather diligent.

Some of the more upmarket hotels may require tourists to pay their bills in foreign currency or show evidence that they have exchanged sufficient money at the bank to pay the bill. If you wish to reconvert your local currency into foreign currency prior to departure, note that it can be a fairly drawn out procedure. One way of avoiding this is to convert only small amounts at a time.

Journalists

If you intend to work as a journalist while in Zimbabwe, it's best not to attempt to hide the fact that you are a journalist. Instead obtain a 24-hour visa before getting accreditation at the Ministry of Home Affairs 11th Floor, Mukwati Building, corner of Fourth Street and Livingstone Avenue, Tel (14) 72-3653, Private Bag 505D Harare.

Health certificates

Your travel agent should be able to tell you which inoculations you may need. Remember to find out at least a month before your visit. Only those visitors coming from cholera or yellow fever areas are required to be in possession of inoculation certificates.

Pets

If you wish to bring a pet into Zimbabwe, contact the Director of Veterinary Services, P. O. Box 8012, Causeway, Harare, well before you leave.

Airport tax

All visitors are required to pay an airport tax of US$10 when leaving by air. The revenue stamp can be purchased before departure at any commercial bank or at the airport.

Manner of dress

There are no dress restrictions in Zimbabwe as long as one remains within the bounds of decency.

Motor vehicles, licences and insurances

In Zimbabwe, driving is on the left-hand side of the road and at uncontrolled intersections you should give way to traffic approaching from the right.

Unless specified to the contrary, the speed limit on open roads is 100 km/h and 60 km/h in urban areas.

All private motor vehicles, trailers and caravans may enter Zimbabwe on condition that they are licensed in their home countries and bear the appropriate registration plates. Zimbabwe recognises the international certificate of motor vehicles. Vehicles must be insured against third party risks. Border posts should be able to supply short-term policies, but contact your insurance broker before departing to make sure.

Cars that are hired from outside Zimbabwe should have appropriate customs surety.

International driving licences as well as driving licences issued in Malawi, South Africa, Zambia, Namibia, Botswana or Swaziland are valid for 90 days. If the licence is not in English it must be accompanied by a certificate of authenticity and validity or a translation of the text into English with an attached and validated photograph of the bearer.

Vehicle spares

Be sure to bring a supply of any spares that you might need as vehicle parts are expensive and in very short supply.

If you are driving into Zimbabwe your emergency spares supply should include fuses, spark plugs, fan-belts, globes, brake and clutch fluid, funnel, thermostat, a water bottle, engine oil, jump leads and a spare set of keys, a tow rope, a puncture kit, spare wheel and tubes, a jack, warning triangles, spare windscreen wiper blades if visiting during the rains, an ignition coil, tyre pressure gauge and pump and distributor points.

5. TRAVELLING INSIDE ZIMBABWE

The two most popular ways of travelling around Zimbabwe are by car and by aeroplane. It is also possible to travel by train and, if you are on Lake Kariba, by boat.

ROAD TRANSPORT

Roads in Zimbabwe

Zimbabwe's road network includes some 5 000 km of first-class bitumen, two-lane roads. When compared with other African countries, Zimbabwe's roads are in excellent condition. The more popular tourist destinations are serviced by superb tarred roads that make driving a pleasure. You don't really need a four-wheel drive vehicle to get anywhere, unless you intend to do some serious "bundu-bashing".

Of course, not all roads are tarred and the gravel roads are usually single-laned and prone to deterioration during the rainy season. Plan your visit well after the rains, so that the road maintenance teams have had a chance to repair any potholes.

As in the United Kingdom, Australia and South Africa, the left-hand drive system is in force and traffic at an unguarded intersection is expected to give way to traffic approaching from the right.

Most roads have distance markers or pegs indicating the distance from a major destination each kilometre. These are very useful as they show you how far you have travelled without having to wait for the next sign to appear.

It is quite possible to do a comfortable round trip of Zimbabwe in under two weeks, taking in all the "must-see" destinations. See the section headed "Standard Routes" below for descriptions of the more popular routes.

Vehicle security

Because new cars are at a premium (importation of cars is limited by severe foreign exchange restrictions), be very aware that if you decide to take your own car into Zimbabwe, it stands a reasonable chance of being stolen. You would therefore be wise to instal effective anti-theft devices in your vehicle before entering the country. Remember to always lock your car.

Vehicle hire

Three major car hire firms are represented in Zimbabwe: Avis, Hertz and Echo-Europcar. These have offices in most of the major tourist spots (see below). A few smaller firms are also in operation.

Agency	Address	Phone
Avis Rent-a-car	**Harare** 5 Samora Machel Ave	(14) 72–0351
	Bulawayo Cnr 10th Avenue/ Robert Mugabe Way	(19) 6–8571
	Bulawayo airport	(19) 2–6657
	Victoria Falls Livingstone Way/ Mellet Drive	(113) 4532
	Kariba Oasis Service Station	(161) 2555
Echo-Europcar	**Harare** 19 Samora Machel Ave P. O. Box 3430	(14) 70–6484
	Sheraton Hotel	(14) 70–0080
	Bulawayo 9a Africa House Fife Street P. O. Box 2320	(19) 6–7925
	Mutare Grants Service Station 1 Crawford Road, Mutare	(120) 6–2367
Fleet Contracts	**Harare** Cnr Leopold Takawira St & Jason Moyo Avenue	(14) 70–5734

Agency	Address	Phone
Hertz Rent-a-car	**Harare** 4 Park Street Monomotapa Hotel Meikles Hotel Airport after hours	(14) 79–3701 (14) 70–4501 (14) 79–3701 (14) 5–0320
	Bulawayo George Silundika St Cnr 14th Avenue	(19) 6–1402
	Bulawayo Airport and a/h	(19) 2–7177
	Victoria Falls Zimbank Building Livingstone Way Airport Victoria Falls Hotel Mutare Publicity Bureau	(113) 4267 43–2522 (113) 3203 (120) 6–4784
	Kariba Cutty Sark Hotel Lake View Hotel Caribbea Bay Hotel	(161) 2321 (161) 2411 (161) 2453
	Masvingo Founders/Robert Mugabe St	(139) 2131
	Hwange Safari Lodge	(118) 393
	Chiredzi Hertz Lowveld Travel	(131) 2295
Truck and Car Hire	Harare 155 Chinhoyi St	(14) 70–0441/2
Taylored Travel	4–wheel drive hire Harare	(14) 88–2287
Royal Car Hire and Tours	Queensway Hatfield	(14) 5–2029

Whichever agency you select, always make sure in advance that it will supply a replacement vehicle if you break down in one of the more inaccessible areas. Also find out how long it will take to get a replacement vehicle to you.

It pays to shop around for the best deal. Before signing a hire contract with any vehicle-hire agency, make sure that essential spares are placed in the vehicle and confirm any existing damage to the bodywork. Also inform the agency of your proposed route and ask whether a four- or two-wheel drive vehicle is necessary for use on that route. If you mislead the company then you must expect to foot the bill for damages that arise if the vehicle is being used over terrain for which it is not suited. Car hire rates in Zimbabwe are high, as spare parts and new vehicles are expensive and hard to obtain because of the tight foreign exchange restrictions. Usually a large cash deposit is required before a car can be hired, but this is waived if payment is by approved credit cards.

The cost of fuel is not usually included in the hire rate, although vehicles may be delivered with a full tank which is filled again at the end of the hiring period so that consumption can be estimated.

The rates of hire cover third-party liability only. Damage to vehicles is considered to be the responsibility of the renter but a collision damage waiver (CDW) may be purchased in advance as a form of insurance. Despite this waiver, the renter is still responsible for damage that is caused to the vehicle by road conditions, negligence or in the case of accident when no other vehicle is involved. If a breakdown does result from the renter's negligence he will be liable for the cost of recovery and rectification.

The driver's minimum age is 21 and some companies impose an upper limit of 65.

Chauffeur and self-drive options are available.

Note that hire vehicles are in short supply in Zimbabwe and you are advised to book yours well before you arrive in the country.

Petrol, diesel and air supply

At the time of writing, petrol was sold throughout the week, usually from 06:00 to 18:00 in the larger centres. There are also a number of 24–hour petrol stations. On the less travelled roads, petrol is still fairly easily available although it may have to be hand-pumped into your car.

There are no grades of petrol, only a blend of petrol and ethanol, a sugar by-product. The ethanol/petrol blend may cause vehicle starting problems in hot weather. A combination of 2–stroke oil and petrol at the rate of 200 ml oil per 50 ℓ petrol may help. Make enquiries regarding the availability of fuel before departing on a trip on secondary or tertiary roads deep in rural areas or inside certain game parks, or keep your tank topped up and carry your own fuel supply. Obtaining air for tyres is not usually a problem.

Buses

In a country short of funds to spend on private vehicles, the bus system is by necessity well developed, reaching into most corners of Zimbabwe. The network is controlled by a handful of private operators who between them offer three levels of service: urban, rural and long distance.

Long distance

Express and Ajay Motorways have coaches that are more tourist-oriented and more comfortable and more expensive than the ordinary, run-of-the-mill bus. If you want a seat on their buses you must book in advance. A luxury coach service runs daily between Bulawayo and Harare and three times a week between Bulawayo and Victoria Falls. Contact Ajay Motorways, Tel Harare (14) 72–8492/72–5673 or Bulawayo (19) 6–2521. Terminals for Ajay are the Bulawayo Sun Hotel in Bulawayo and the Monomatapa Hotel in Harare. Express Motorways are at the coach terminal, Rezende Street, Harare, Tel (14) 72–0392. In Bulawayo book through Musgrove and Watson, in Mutare book through Tourist Information.

Urban

This is a less reliable, far more crowded means of getting around, the buses are less punctual and time is wasted standing in queues. Rather use the taxi system.

Rural

The rural bus services link the main centres with country areas. The ordinary rural buses are cheap but extremely slow and liable to breakdown. If you use them, allow yourself plenty of time.

Hitchhiking

This is said to be a relatively easy way of getting round Zimbabwe. Some of those who offer lifts will be unofficial taxis and expect payment. Check what is expected before accepting a ride.

When hitching over long distances, it helps if you prepare a card with your destination written clearly on it to hold up for passing motorists to see. Always remember to choose a safe place where drivers can pull off the road without any risk to themselves from passing traffic. The more luggage you are carrying, the less chance you have of getting a lift.

Cycling

If you are planning a biking holiday it is advisable to bring your own bike, although it is possible to hire bikes at Pedalpushers, 46 Samora Machel Avenue, Harare, next to Livingstone House, Tel (14) 70-2069 and 30-4422. They also have a base at Victoria Falls.

For spares and repairs in Harare try also Zacks Cycle Co., in Vanguard House on Kenneth Kaunda Avenue opposite the railway station, and Manica Cycle Company on the corner of Robert Mugabe Road and Second Street, Tel 72-2216. In Bulawayo, try Royal Cycle Suppliers, corner of Robert Mugabe Way and 10th Avenue, Tel (19) 6-9168.

Unless you enjoy sweltering heat, plan your holiday to coincide with the cooler dry months of May, June, July and August. Winds are usually easterly and not very strong. The hot, dry months of September and October are the windiest months of the year.

If you do bring your own bike, remember to pack a good supply of spares as they are expensive and not readily available in Zimbabwe.

Bring the following spares:

three-way socket spanner	inner tube
flat multi-hole spanner	screwdriver
adjustable spanner	brake cable
grease	pump
rear gear cable	Allen keys
brake blocks	chain links
bulbs	spokes
ball bearings	small nuts and bolts
cone spanner	chain rivet tool
oil	freewheel remover
spoke nipple key	small nail punch
pedal dustcap spanner	small pliers
cotterless crank remover spanner	pvc insulating tape
puncture kit	

If you wish to obtain a fact sheet on cycling in Zimbabwe, send a stamped addressed envelope to the Cyclists Touring Club, Cotterell House, 69 Meadrow, Godalming, Surrey, GU7 3HS.

Taxis

Taxi ranks are found outside the larger hotels in the major centres and at Bulawayo and Harare airports. A ten per cent tip is usually expected. Taxi meters are not subject to rigorous police control and hence prices may vary over the same distance.

A1 Taxis	Tel Harare (14) 70–6996
Avondale	Tel Harare (14) 3–5883
Creamline	Tel Harare (14) 70–3333
Rixi	Tel Harare (14) 70–7707

Safari operators

See list on page 79.

Speed limits

Unless otherwise specified, limits in rural areas are 100 km/h and in urban areas, 60 km/h.

Driving etiquette

Zimbabwean drivers display no peculiarities, except for the occasional signalling with indicators whether it is safe to overtake or not. If it is not safe they indicate with the right indicator; if it is safe, with the left. Bear in mind though that you bear the ultimate responsibility for judging whether it is safe to overtake or not.

Although large trucks are supposed to adhere to the speed limits, they tend to ignore these if given a clear and flattish stretch of road.

Maps and name changes

After independence Zimbabwe Africanised many street and place names. To avoid confusion, make sure that you have the latest maps (see below). Your best bet is the AA, Fanum House, Samora Machel Avenue, Harare, Tel (14) 70-7021 (see page 111) or try the department of the Surveyor General, Electra House, Samora Machel Avenue, P. O. Box 8099, Causeway, Tel (14) 79-4545.

Names of towns and settlements that have changed:

New	Old
Chegutu	Hartley
Chimanimani	Melsetter
Chinhoyi	Sinoia
Chipinge	Chipinga
Chivhu	Enkeldoorn
Dete	Dett
Esigodini	Essexvale
Gweru	Gwelo
Guruwe	Sipolilo
Kadoma	Gatooma
Kwekwe	Que Que
Harare	Salisbury
Hwange	Wankie
Hurungwe	Urungue
Marondera	Marandellas
Mashava	Mashaba
Masvingo	Fort Victoria
Matobo	Matopos
Mazowe	Mazoe
Mbalabala	Balla Balla
Mberengwa	Belingwe
Mhangura	Mangula
Munyati	Umniati
Murewa	Mrewa
Mutare	Umtali
Mutepatepa	Matepatepa
Mutoko	Mtoko
Mutorashanga	Mtoroshanga
Mvurwi	Umvukwes
Mvuma	Umvuma
Mwenezi	Nuanetsi
Ngezi	Ingezi
Nkayi	Nkai
Nyanga	Inyanga
Nyazura	Inyazura
Sango	Vila Salazar
Shurugwi	Selukwe
Somabhula	Somabula
Tsholotsho	Tjolotjo
Zvishavane	Shabani

Rivers

The names of many rivers have also been changed. The more important are listed below.

Bubi	Bubyi
Gwayi	Gwaai
Khame	Khami
Manyame	Hunyani
Mutilikwe	Mtelikwe
Munyati	Umniati
Mupfure	Umfuri
Mwenezi	Nuanetsi
Runde	Lundi
Save	Sabi
Thuli	Tuli

Street names

Harare

Simon Mazorodze Way	Beatrice Road, Watt Road/Chandler Way
Robson Manyika Avenue	Forbes Avenue
Bishop Gaul Avenue	Gaul Avenue
George Silundika Avenue	Gordon Avenue
Harare Road	Harare Road North
Masvingo Road	Harare/Beatrice Rd
Seke Road	Hatfield Road/Prince Edward Dam Road
Samora Machel Avenue	Jameson Avenue
Robert Mugabe Way	Manica Road
Mazowe St	Mazoe St
Leopold Takawira St	Moffat St
Josiah Chinamano Road	Montague Avenue
Mutoko Road	Mtoko Road
Josiah Tongogara Avenue	North Avenue
Kaguvi Street	Pioneer Street
Airport Road	Queensway North/Queensway Road
Herbert Chitepo Avenue	Rhodes Avenue

Harare Drive
Harare Street
Harare Way
Chinhoyi Street
Rekayi Tangwena Avenue
Jason Moyo Avenue
Mutare Road
Mbuya Nehanda St
Chiremba Road

Salisbury Drive
Salisbury Street
Salisbury Way
Sinoia Street
Sir James Macdonald Ave
Stanley Avenue
Umtali Road
Victoria St
Widdecombe Road

Bulawayo

Jason Moyo Street
Samuel Parirenyatwa St
Robert Mugabe Way
Herbert Chitepo St
Plumtree Road
Masotsha Ndlovu Ave
Josiah Chinamano Road
Gwanda Road

Abercorn Street
Borrow Street
Grey Street
Jameson Street
Mafeking Road
Kings Avenue
London Road
Birchenough Road/
Queens Road to Airport/
Johannesburg Road

Robert Mugabe Way
George Silundika Street
Harare Road
Leopold Takawira Avenue
Josiah Tongogara Street

Queens Road
Rhodes Street
Salisbury Road
Selborne Avenue
Wilson Street

Mutare

Leopold Takawira Road
Independence Avenue
Chaminuka Way
Herbert Chitepo Street
Robert Mugabe Avenue

Allan Wilson Road
Cecil Avenue
Kings Way
Main Street
Churchill Road/
Miller Avenue

Aerodrome Road

Aerodrome Road/
Victoria Avenue

Simon Mazoredze Road
Jason Moyo Drive
Tembwe Street
Bvumba Avenue

Meikle Road
Rhodes Drive
Turner Street
Vumba Avenue

The Automobile Association of Zimbabwe (AAZ)

The AA (Automobile Association) can supply you with a detailed and up-to-date map of Zimbabwe and a number of national parks.

Harare	Fanum House Samora Machel Ave P. O. Box 585 Harare Tel (14) 70–7021 Open from 07:30 to 16:30
Bulawayo	Fanum House Cnr Leopold Takawira Ave and Josiah Tongogara St Tel (19) 7–0063
Gweru	Fanum House Cnr Lobengula Avenue and Sixth Street Tel (154) 4251
Mutare	Fanum House 10 Robert Mugabe Ave Tel (120) 64422

There are also offices at Beitbridge, Bindura, Chinhoyi, Chipinge, Chiredzi, Hwange, Kadoma, Kariba, Kwekwe, Karoi, Marondera, Masvingo, Rusape, Victoria Falls and Zvishavane.

The subscription and membership rates for the AAZ are extremely reasonable and in return the motorist is entitled to free technical advice, maps and touring documents, legal advice and defence, breakdown service, emergency hotel expenses and a car unlocking service. Subsidised services include hotel bookings, triptyques and carnets, emergency travel expenses scheme, emergency aid vouchers and technical inspections. Membership of the AA also means that you can get discounts and special rates at most major hotels in Zimbabwe, on motor insurance, on a visa service and on shipping and railage of cars.

Accidents and driving hazards

If there are no serious injuries to any parties involved in the accident and the vehicles are causing an obstruction in the road, then they may be moved to the side of the road and the police notified within 24 hours. Otherwise police should be notified immediately.

In most parts of the country, livestock are fenced off from the main roads in rural areas. There are communal farming areas where there are no fences, but where animals are usually kept well under control by herders. Roads and verges are extremely well maintained and all road signs conform to accepted Western norms. Once outside the cities, there is little traffic. Despite this, however, it is advisable not to travel at night.

STANDARD ROUTES

Once you have decided which parts of Zimbabwe you wish to visit, you will need to plan your route in more detail. While bearing in mind that the quality of untarred roads changes with the season, decide whether to use a four-wheel-drive vehicle or not, particularly if you plan to visit the more remote destinations during or just after the wet season.

The descriptions of routes and the length of time it takes to get from place to place are subjective and will vary depending on speed conditions. Please regard these descriptions more as guidelines than hard and fast rules.

Only the more commonly used tourist routes are described in this section.

The following descriptions indicate in brief what you can expect to see on some of the most popular routes in Zimbabwe, working in a clockwise direction with Harare as the starting point. All roads are in excellent condition unless otherwise stated.

Route 1 – Harare to Nyanga

(The figures in brackets indicate the distance between that place and the next.)

Distances:

Harare – Marondera   74 km   (96 km)
       – Rusape   170 km (69 km)
       – Juliasdale 239 km (29 km)
       – Nyanga   268 km

Leave Harare by the Mutare Road, which is also the road to the airport turn off and to Mukuvisi woodlands. Turn right at Glenara Avenue South, about 3 km from the city centre. The road becomes the A3.

For quite a distance the road follows the railway line as it passes through pleasant, flattish terrain composed mainly of large estates and a few smallholdings. There are a number of roadside kiosks selling all manner of interesting fresh produce, which is very useful if you plan to do your own catering. Some of the delicacies that can be bought include fresh asparagus, honey, goatsmilk cheese, peaches, oranges, fresh milk, cream and mushrooms. Among the exotic trees such as bluegums, pines and jacarandas, the image of raw Africa is not uppermost. There remain strong pointers to Zimbabwe's colonial past, especially in the profusion of English names. At a distance of 70 km outside Harare, you will pass the turn off to Imire Game Park, which is some 37 km further.

The town of Marondera (Marandellas in the colonial past) is a little further on, at 74 km from Harare.

The main street of this small sleepy town is lined with small shops and a garage. The Marondera Hotel is situated just off the main road. One of the most memorable aspects of the area is the stunning contrast between the startling violet, pink, lilac and purple hues of the bougainvillea and jacarandas that grow in the vicinity.

After Marondera, the flatlands begin to drop away to the sides of the road, which runs along on a kind of spinal ridge surrounded by wide open acres of fenced farmland. The names that appear on the side of the road suggest a broad cultural mix that is dominated by English, Afrikaans and Shona.

At 135 km from Harare in the midst of cattle-ranching country is the turn off to Headlands, a small village with a hotel just 2 km from the main road. The scenery stretching away to either side of the road is hilly, with huge boulders balanced precariously on each other here and there. The overriding image is of a giant's playground with the boulders being the marbles that the giants have tossed around during their games. Small collections of round thatched huts contained within a makeshift "kraal" or enclosure may also be seen.

Some 35 km further on the entrance to Rusape is marked by the Crocodile Hotel on your left. Driving into the centre of this small, neat and quiet tree-lined town you will see the Balfour Hotel. You have to turn left in the centre of the town to follow the road to Nyanga (99 km). Just as you leave town you will see the turn off to Diana's Vow rock paintings (30 km). From here the distance to Juliasdale, a town en route to Nyanga, is 78 km.

Sixteen kilometres outside Rusape you notice that in the distance the terrain begins to change markedly. It is only at this point that you get the feeling you are heading for the Eastern Highlands. You pass intriguing hill shapes, and peculiar rock formations with sharp vertical and horizontal cracks in them. There are more and more huts and unfenced grazing areas on communally owned land. Watch out for cows on the road at this point and, indeed, wherever you notice the absence of fencing. The cows are usually kept well under control by herders but the odd one sometimes decides to go its own way.

Seventy kilometres outside Rusape the scenery becomes more spectacular and montane as the road winds in and out of pine forest. This is the area known as Juliasdale, which is not so much a town but a collection of hotels. Here you will find to the right and left of the road such notables as the Brondesbury Park Hotel (page 145) the Montclair Casino Hotel and the Pinetree Inn. There is also a butchery and a 24-hour petrol service station and notice listing the names of those who are fortunate enough to own retirement homes in the area. From here it is 20 km to Nyanga. There is also a turnoff to Mutare (84 km) to the south.

About 8 km beyond Juliasdale you'll pass the entrance to Nyanga National Park on your right. From the entrance, the park office is some 4 km further on. Continuing through the rolling hills and forest, you pass the turn off to Udu Dam to the left, and Nyangombe campsite (visible just off the road) to the right.

Six kilometres on is the turn off to Troutbeck (15 km). If you are heading to Nyanga town, you continue on the excellent tarred road traversing the national park, to the settlement nestling at the foot of the surrounding mountains.

To reach Troutbeck the road twists and turns through Nyanga National Park land for some distance before descending slightly into pine and wattle plantations and the tiny settlement of Troutbeck which is almost adjacent to the Troutbeck Inn entrance.

Route 2 – Nyanga to Mutare

Distance: Nyanga–Mutare 105 km

There are two ways of reaching Mutare. You can choose to return to Juliasdale and turn left (84 km), or you can travel through the Nyanga National Park on the Scenic Road taking in Mtarazi Falls and Pungwe

Falls. Whichever you take you are guaranteed an up-hill, down-dale experience, with pine forests flanking the road for much of the way. Hills tumble over themselves in the distance as you cross and re-cross the meandering Odzi River. The road from Pungwe Gorge and the Honde Valley meets the A15 to Mutare at the 61 km point. If you have time travel down the Honde Valley road and visit the old-fashioned clubhouse of the Aberfoyle tea estates, where it is also possible to stay overnight. As you descend into the Honde Valley, the views are spectacular.

Leaving the pine forests, you enter a communal farming area which proves to be a very sad sight. Huge erosion scars are everywhere and bare, red earth stretches far into the distance. Wherever you look, the land is suffering.

The turn off to Penhalonga is 41 km outside Mutare. From the A15 it is a distance of 30 km.

As you get closer to Mutare, the land becomes greener and there is evidence of irrigation. Passing old Mutare, which is nothing like new Mutare, there is another turn off to Penhalonga about 8 km outside town. Then you climb the Christmas Pass driving by an unprepossessing hotel on the right of the road. The pass itself is not that steep but as it begins to descend there is a spectacular view of Mutare on the valley floor surrounded by mountains all around.

The city is like most other Zimbabwean cities and towns; clean and well laid out with wide open streets, some so wide that you feel lost on the island in the middle while waiting to cross over.

Route 3 – Mutare to Chimanimani

Distance: Mutare–Chimanimani 150 km

When leaving Mutare and heading for Chimanimani be sure to take the Chimanimani road out of town rather than the signposted route past the publicity association, which takes you to the border post and the Vumba Mountains.

It takes longer to get to Chimanimani than the distance would indicate. On the map it looks a relatively short distance, but the road is winding and hilly, necessitating frequent gear changes in places and a relatively slow speed, so that the trip takes more than three hours.

After leaving Mutare the road goes through very arid country and communal farming lands, again very badly affected by erosion, skirting the foothills of the Eastern Highland ramparts. The grass is very sparse and all that arrests the attention are some tortuously shaped rocks and boulders and hills.

Sixty-seven kilometres from Mutare the road to Cashel, a fertile fruit and vegetable growing area in the east, leaves the A9 at Wengezi Junction and heads towards the mountains while following the course of the Umvumvumvu River and sometimes crossing it. The appearance of mango trees signals a change in climate and transition to lowveld vegetation.

As you turn off onto the road to Chimanimani 15 km from Wengezi Junction, the road continues through communal farmland. This seems to be a very desolate part of Zimbabwe, somewhat isolated. The dry red earth produces hardly a blade of grass. One wonders how people and their animals survive in this harsh, inhospitable landscape. There is very little, if any, evidence of modern development, just a few small African villages that must have been the same for hundreds of years.

After some 60 km of winding road, with a backdrop of fairly high but undramatic mountains in the distance towards the east, the road starts rising steeply and all of a sudden you are in pine and bluegum country again, the harsh red earth forgotten. At the summit of this climb just as you reach the Skyline Junction where the road splits, changing direction for Chipinge and ultimately Masvingo, there is a magnificent view of Chimanimani, way in the distance, a tiny speck nestling at the foot of the Chimanimani Mountains. From here the drive winds down some 19 km to the small settlement, which provides good access to the Bridal Veil Falls, the Chimanimani National Park and the Chimanimani Eland Sanctuary.

Route 4 – Chimanimani to Masvingo

Distances:

Chimanimani – Skyline Junction   19 km
    – Chipinge   68 km
    – Birchenough Bridge   106 km
    – Masvingo   278 km

From the Skyline Junction turning to Chipinge, the road winds down slowly till eventually from montane forest you are back in the land of the baobab, the lowveld, a harsh, dry, inhospitable land peppered with a few irrigated farms that serve to punctuate the stark landscape.

From the Chipinge turn off it is 51 km to the A9 from Mutare just before it veers to the west over the wide Save River by means of the very large, incongruous, silver-spidery Birchenough Bridge that unexpectedly rises out of nowhere.

The settlement of Birchenough Bridge is small enough to miss as you pass by in a hurry, but if you need to stop there is a hotel and petrol pump.

The A9 continues through the lowlands, rising very slightly into Masvingo Province. As far as the eye can see are slowly undulating hills, covered by grey-green scrub and trees. Most of the land is fenced, indicating the boundaries of the giant ranches that comprise tens of thousands of acres.

All that interrupts the vastness of the landscape is several interesting rock formations and giant-strewn boulders. There are cows on the road with massive horns and passing buses with quaint names such as "The Prodigal Son", improbably loaded with beds and dining-room tables on their roof carriers. There are also well-dressed school children, spick and span in their school uniforms. Some of the traditional Ndebele huts are attractively decorated with two or three shades of ochre in designs not seen in other parts of Zimbabwe.

Again, in this part of the world, there seems to have been very little colonial influence and the territory is sparsely populated. The communal farm-lands are very evident by their obvious over-grazing and erosion.

Twenty-seven kilometres before Masvingo is one of two turn offs to Lake Mutirikwi (formerly Lake Kyle). This turn off leads to the northern part of the lake and offers an alternative route past the dam wall, through to the Mutirikwe Lakeshore lodges, Kyle View chalets and Great Zimbabwe, if you wish to avoid going through Masvingo.

Just 13 km from Masvingo is a second turn off to the lake (19 km) which takes you to the national parks lodges and campsite within the game park.

Masvingo is a sleepy town with many links to the colonial past. Although it is somewhat off the beaten track there is no evidence of decay. Everything is clean and neat. You enter and leave via a wide four-laned road flanked by shops that could supply most of your immediate needs. The distance from Masvingo to the ruins is a reasonable 26 km if you prefer to stay in town, or if accommodation is not available at Great Zimbabwe Hotel, which is adjacent to the ruins.

Route 5 – Masvingo to Bulawayo

Distances:

Masvingo – Zvishavane   97 km
          – Bulawayo   280 km

To leave Masvingo head out on Josiah Tongogara Road till you find the sign indicating a turn off to the left for Bulawayo. For quite a distance the scenery along this route consists of parched, arid scrub, dry river beds and plenty of leafless trees that create a grey fuzz on the landscape.

Here and there you will spot evidence that mines are operating in the vicinity. Names like Fred Mine, King Mine, Vanguard Mine and Croft Mine crop up. Again, you feel pity for the animals standing forlornly on the side of the road, and wonder how they manage to salvage even a blade of grass from this hostile landscape.

Be warned that if you have children in the car, this is a long and uneventful drive (apart from the regular sightings of monkeys and baboons) and you should stock up with diversions to take their minds off the three-hour journey. Don't rely on the radio, as reception is not up to much here.

You will pass Zvishavane, a tiny mining town with the Hotel Nilton smack bang in its centre.

Now and again you will notice the remains of the old strip road in the bush on the side of the road. Sections of it have been partially excavated. You marvel at the superb condition of the two-lane A9 and wonder how long it must have taken to travel between Masvingo and Bulawayo when there was only a strip road.

At Mbalabala, 119 km from Masvingo, the A9 joins the A6 Bulawayo-Beitbridge road. It is just 65 km from Bulawayo and the site of a large army base. There is also a 24-hour petrol station.

At Esigodini, 43 km from Bulawayo, you notice the start of irrigated lands and large-scale cultivation as you start climbing the escarpment to Bulawayo. The entire Bulawayo/Masvingo area has been ravaged by a drought for nearly ten years. Some rain falls every year but not nearly enough. Bulawayo suffers from drastic water restrictions and plans have been made to build a water pipeline from the Zambezi in the north, but at the time of writing, costs were prohibitive.

Twenty-five kilometres outside Bulawayo is the signpost for the Chipangali animal orphanage and wildlife trust (see page 24). As you approach Bulawayo, you can see some of the taller buildings rising up out of the plain in the distance. You pass scattered houses lining the road and the Hilltop Motel some 3 km from this sleepy, quiet city that rivals Harare in many people's affections.

Sunglasses are a must for Bulawayo as the sun seems to drench the place, soaking into every corner of this wide open and friendly city of approximately 500 000 inhabitants.

To get to Matobo National Park, you need to traverse Bulawayo and travel some 25 km to the south-west of the city.

Route 6 – Bulawayo to Victoria Falls

Distances:
Bulawayo – Hwange National Park   261 km
         – Victoria Falls   439 km

Leave Bulawayo for Victoria Falls via Lady Stanley Avenue, which leads to the north-west. Some 60 km from the city you'll notice much larger trees than you've seen up to now, and they will also be denser and closer to the side of the road. They present a very much more attractive aspect than the grey scrubland of the south. There is also substantially more grass.

Although there is not much evidence of human habitation, now and again you will see small groups of people waiting patiently on the side of the road for a bus.

The road is long and straight through this flattish but pleasant countryside. At about 200 km from Bulawayo, the road drops ever so gently to the lowveld with its green, dense vegetation. Deforestation does not seem to be too much of a problem here when compared with other parts of Zimbabwe. At the 254 km peg is the turn off to Sikumi Tree Lodge, which is a further 25 km off the road.

Near the 258 km peg you will see a sign warning motorists of elephants crossing the road. This is a sure indication that you are nearing Hwange National Park.

Just 2 km further on is the turn off to Main Camp (23 km from the main road) and Hwange Safari Lodge (11 km from the main road).

As you travel into the park, note the fairly obvious change in vegetation. Also note that there is fuel at Hwange Safari Lodge and at Main Camp.

Continuing towards Victoria Falls the distance from the turn off to Main Camp to Hwange town is 70 km and to Victoria Falls 172 km.

About 20 km from this turn off, or at the 281 km peg, is the turn off to Mlibizi (95 km) which is the terminus for the *Sealion* ferry that crosses Lake Kariba and docks in Kariba.

As you drive north, the terrain becomes much hillier and the baobab makes its appearance in its preferred hot and arid habitat. At the 331 km peg you pass the turn off to Sinamatella Camp in the Hwange National Park.

Hwange's power station chimneys come into view before the town itself is visible. The road bypasses Hwange, although there is a petrol station and small supply store on the side of the road for those who need to fill up.

Just 6 km out of Hwange is the turn off to the right to Deka, which is 48 km away.

Some 60 km beyond Hwange is the turn off to Robins Camp and Nantwich Camp in the Hwange National Park. The same road leads to Matetsi Safari Area (25 km) and then to Pandamatenga border post, 64 km away on the Botswana border.

All along this road you'll have to dodge the baboons, warthogs and guinea fowl, which are so used to the traffic they barely turn a hair as you drive past.

As you get closer to Victoria Falls you will notice a few curio stalls on the side of the road. It's worth stopping here as prices are lower than at the busier curio stalls in town.

Twenty-one kilometres from Victoria Falls is the turn off to the airport and at the 425 km peg there is yet another turn off to Deka but this route is longer (109 km) than the one previously mentioned.

Entering Victoria Falls is like arriving at the seaside. You expect that, like the sea, the falls will be impossible to miss and as you drive into the central business district you peer through the vegetation and buildings on the side of the road to catch a glimpse of them. In fact, the road into the town leads straight to the falls, which you will reach if you continue through the town. This road eventually ends at the border post with Zambia.

Route 7 – Victoria Falls to Kariba

There are several ways of reaching Kariba from Victoria Falls. One very pleasant way is to load your car onto the ferry that departs from Mlibizi (191 km from Victoria Falls) and take the relaxing 22-hour journey to Kariba (see page 125). However, if you intend to do this trip you must make sure that you book your passage well in advance.

This will save you the long return journey (1 245 km) by road from Kariba back to Bulawayo and from there north to Kariba via Harare and Makuti. If you wish to go bushwhacking you could cut across from Harare to the south of Lake Kariba but you would have to carry your own fuel over uncertain and isolated terrain.

Route 8 – Kariba to Harare

Distances:
Kariba – Harare   366 km
Kariba – Makuti   79 km
Makuti – Harare   292 km

Leaving Kariba, the road passes the turn off to the airport some 18 km from the town and the turn offs to the Nyanyana camping site and the crocodile park.

The road starts winding through hilly terrain which comprises game reserve land. Hence you may come across elephant droppings or even the great beasts themselves. Don't be surprised if you turn a corner and bump into a herd of buffalo. Although you cannot drive at high speed because of the hilly terrain, it pays to be extra vigilant for the wild animals that may unexpectedly dash into your path.

For some 37 km the road continues through the park before a sign announces that you have passed through the reserve's boundaries. Just before the rains the terrain is parched, thirstily awaiting the moisture that will bring a covering of green to the stony soil. In springtime magnificent trees with bright scarlet blooms add a touch of colour to this intriguing landscape.

The road is in excellent condition but you will notice no sign of human habitation between Kariba and Makuti. Makuti, situated on the plateau some 77 km from Kariba, is at the road's summit and offers magnificent but hazy views over the surrounding terrain, stretching into the distance. On a clear day it is said that you can see Lake Kariba.

If you want to stop for refreshments in Makuti, your best and only bet is the Cloud's End Hotel which is conveniently situated at the Kariba/Harare and Chirundu/Harare junction. It is a popular and convenient overnight choice for travellers heading for the northern border as the short distance between Makuti and the border (60 km) ensures that they can be at the border very early the next morning.

The road between Makuti and Harare runs along the plateau, so the gently undulating terrain holds no surprises. Most of the farms lining the road are neatly fenced and are obviously of great size. Most of them are under large-scale maize and tobacco cultivation, and you will see the occasional tobacco curing sheds. The vegetation is savanna grassland for most of the journey with relatively sparse tree growth.

The first large town encountered is Karoi, which is neat and ordered. There are a few garages, some shops along the main road and Karoi Hotel.

From there the road stretches out like a long ribbon for miles ahead to Chinhoyi, the next major town before Harare. The scenery is still very much the same, rather unsurprising, but very evocative of Zimbabwe's handsomeness. You'll see the odd herd of cattle, bright green patches of irrigated tobacco and some grain storage silos.

Before you enter the town of Chinhoyi you'll pass the Chinhoyi Caves and Caves Motel. If you have time and are interested in caves, it is worth stopping for a short visit. It is possible to camp at the site which just borders the caves.

Chinhoyi is a reasonably large town but you do not need to stop off here unless you are visiting friends or doing business. If you are heading for Bulawayo or Beitbridge, you can take the turn off to Chegutu to the south which bypasses Harare.

The remainder of the route to Harare is unspectacular. The land to either side of the road becomes imperceptibly more built up as you get closer to Harare.

Route 9 – Bulawayo to Harare

Distances:

Bulawayo – Gweru   164 km (Distance to next town 62 km)
         – Kwekwe 226 km (72 km)
         – Kadoma 298 km (34 km)
         – Chegutu 332 km (107 km)
         – Harare   439 km

For some distance outside Bulawayo the landscape is flat and generally featureless, although it is not as arid and inhospitable looking as the more southerly portions of Zimbabwe can be.

The A5 follows the direction of the Great Dyke, the raised spinal portion that makes up the "highveld" region of Zimbabwe, stretching from the south-west to the north-east.

Just outside Shangani, a tiny town 81 km from Bulawayo, you'll pass the turn offs to Danangombe and Naletale ruins, said by many to rival the Khame ruins further south. Closer to Gweru, farms increase in number on either side of the road. On the other side of Gweru, which rivals Mutare as Zimbabwe's third city in terms of size and facilities, you'll notice that trees are more plentiful. Most of the land on either side of the road belongs to the huge cattle ranches of the highveld.

AIR TRANSPORT

There are daily flights between major centres and tourist resorts. The national carrier Air Zimbabwe flies between Harare and Bulawayo, Victoria Falls, Kariba, Masvingo and Gweru. It also flies to Hwange via Kariba and Buffalo Range via Masvingo.

Harare airport is 18 km from the city and there is a regular Air Zimbabwe bus service. The same applies to Bulawayo airport, which is 22 km from Bulawayo. Other destinations are serviced by private touring companies that can provide transfers between the airport and nearest hotels.

Charter flights can also be arranged through private companies and safari operators. Charles Prince Airport, situated about 18 km north-west of Harare, is the capital's second airport. Zimbabwe's light aircraft industry is based here, together with a flying school and the Mashonaland Flying Club. Charles Prince Airport, P. O. Box HG300, Highlands, Harare, Tel (14) 79–6361.

Some of the private charter companies in operation in Zimbabwe include:
Executive Air
P. O. Box EH96, Emerald Hill, Harare, Tel (14) 3–2959/3–2999 and United Air Charters
P. O. Box AP50, Harare Airport, Harare, Tel (14) 73–7317
Victoria Falls Tel (113) 4530/4220,
Kariba, Tel (161) 2321/2 (this company operates the "Flight of Angels" trip over the Victoria Falls).

Air Zimbabwe offers tourists a package called the Flame Lily Holiday which is extremely good value for money. The choice of destinations and the time spent at each is very flexible and the package is inclusive of flights, first class hotel accommodation, meals, excursions and transfer fares to Hwange, Great Zimbabwe, Victoria Falls and Kariba. It is best to purchase the packages in your home country.

RAIL TRANSPORT

The National Railways of Zimbabwe (NRZ) runs a 3 400 km rail network which connects all the larger towns and cities. First and second class are more expensive and comfortable than third and fourth class, which are extremely cheap. However, not all trains have third and fourth class coaches.

The network is being electrified although some diesel locos and about 95 steam locomotives are still in use.

If you want to take a trip by train, book as far in advance as possible. Bookings for internal trips open 30 days in advance while those to destinations outside Zimbabwe open 90 days in advance. National Railways of Zimbabwe, P. O. Box 582 Harare, Tel (14) 70–0033. Trains travelling overnight offer sleeper services where bedding and mattresses can be hired. Buy your bedding tickets at the station when you buy your train ticket.

Two-, four- or six-berth compartments are available with the *coupe* (two-berth) being most suitable for a couple and four or six berths either going to families or passengers of the same sex.

If you are a steam fanatic, don't miss the overnight trip from Bulawayo to Victoria Falls (see Rail safaris, page 78). Contact Rail Safaris, Chancellor House, Samora Machel Avenue, Harare, P. O Box 4070 Harare, Tel (14) 73–6056.

BOAT TRANSPORT

All kinds of small boats ply the waters of Lake Kariba, cramming the marinas at Kariba and giving the visitor the impression that he has somehow dropped into the French Riviera. Of the larger boats, Kariba Ferries operates a 22–hour, one-way return service between Kariba and Mlibizi, saving over 1 250 km of driving if your aim is to get to Harare from Victoria Falls or the other way round. They will also ferry your car and caravan if you book well in advance. You stand a chance of getting on if you just turn up and there has been a cancellation. However, the journey is more difficult from the Victoria Falls end of the lake as the trip between the falls and Mlibizi takes some three and a half hours. It takes you off the beaten track, so it is not really worth hours of travel just to arrive and find that there is no space on the boat for your car.

The company running the ferry will not confirm a booking until it has received a deposit. Final payment for the trip is due 14 days before the date of sailing.

The *Sealion* ferry has a windowed saloon, an open deck and a large shaded upper lounge deck. A full bar service is available on board and the tariff includes meals, tea and coffee. You sleep in comfortable airline-type chairs. Be sure to take along a pair of binoculars to view game on the shore. Also remember a hat, sunscreen and towels.

Boat charter companies are mostly based at Kariba and a few have offices in Harare.

Company	Address	Telephone number
Anchorage Marina	P. O. Box 61 Kariba	(161) 246
Blue Water Charters	P. O. Box 78 Kariba	(161) 2971/2
Chessa	P. O. Box X774 Harare	(14) 4–6684/6–4032
Kariba Breezes Marina	P. O. Box 15 Kariba	(161) 2475
Kariba Marine Charters	P. O. Box CH169 Chisipite, Harare	
Kariba Yacht Safaris	Cutty Sark Hotel, Kariba	(161) 2321

Sailing safaris
See page 77.

6. FACTORS AFFECTING HOLIDAY PLANNING

SEASONS AND CLIMATE

Although the country lies within the tropics, it does not have the steamy temperatures and lush vegetation usually associated with the term "tropical". This can be largely explained by Zimbabwe's topographical make up.

The country's high-lying central plateau and Eastern Highlands have fairly cool year-round temperatures. Conversely in the lower-lying areas such as the Zambezi River Valley, Victoria Falls and Kariba, Hwange and Gonarezhou national parks, temperatures and humidity are very high in the hot season, and winters are fairly warm.

The fact that Zimbabwe is so far inland helps to reduce the humidity levels to a certain extent. As it is south of the equator, the seasons are the opposite to those in the northern hemisphere. Very broadly speaking the seasons can be divided into summer and winter with summer beginning in October and lasting till about March while winter can be said to begin in May with a peak in June, July and August with the start of the spring transition to summer in September. Mean daytime summer temperatures are from 25–30 °C while mean daytime winter temperatures are about 15–20 °C.

The dry season coincides with the cooler weather and most of the country experiences drought until the rains begin in early November. October is known as "suicide month" as temperatures build up sharply without the relief of rain.

A month-by-month breakdown

April

You could call this pivotal month "Autumn" in that temperatures start dropping and rainfall decreases markedly.

May

The start of winter in May is pleasant with warm days and cool nights.

Factors affecting holiday planning

June, July and August

Relatively cold but still mild by European standards. Some wind and cloud. The countryside becomes drab and brown from lack of rain, and occasional frosts occur on higher ground. Night temperatures drop to below freezing.

September

Spring's arrival is heralded by the first warm days and the burgeoning of new vegetation.

October

Uncomfortably hot and dry with jacarandas and flamboyant trees in full bloom – spring has indeed sprung by now. If the heat bothers you, plan your visit for another month as temperatures often exceed 30 °C.

November

The start of the rains brings some welcome relief from the hot temperatures.

December, January, February and March

Temperatures are still high but there are frequent brief, heavy showers and thunderstorms, with some spells of overcast weather. Nights are cooler.

Best times to visit national parks and botanical reserves

The dry season is best for game viewing as water supplies dwindle and game is forced to congregate around remaining waterholes rather than dispersing over a wide area. The peak of the dry season, October, coincides with the lowest water supplies and consequently the highest game concentrations.

Note that the Victoria Falls are at their best between February and May. The best time to visit the lowveld (i.e. Mana Pools, Victoria Falls, Kariba) is during the more temperate months of spring and autumn (August-September/March-April).

You should also be aware that towards the end of the rains and during the early and cooler part of the dry season, the grass is long and likely to obscure your view of the game. It is only towards the end of the dry season that most of the available grass has been eaten and/or trampled, resulting in superior visibility.

HEALTH PRECAUTIONS

Zimbabwe's medical facilities are adequate for most illnesses and emergencies, but cases requiring specialised treatment are usually referred to South Africa or the United Kingdom.

Bulawayo, Harare, Gweru and Mutare all have large general hospitals and doctors and dentists in private practice. The names, addresses and telephone numbers of medical practitioners are printed in the front of the telephone books before the alphabetical listings begin.

Visitors who are undergoing treatment for any disorders are advised to take adequate supplies of specialised drugs they may require.

It's worth knowing about the most common tropical ailments specific to Zimbabwe, though there's no reason to be alarmed as the chances are that your visit will be trouble-free in health terms. Regard this section merely as a handy reference, particularly for those who intend to travel along the less well-trodden paths.

It is worthwhile taking out medical insurance before arriving.

Obtaining medical help

To obtain emergency assistance in Harare, Bulawayo, Mutare, Nyanga and Hwange areas dial 99. To find a hospital check in the phone directory under "important numbers".

Malaria

Malaria is confined to certain low-lying parts of Zimbabwe. The most prevalent strain of the malaria parasite is *P. falciparum*.

If you are travelling around the country you will probably pass through some malarial areas. As a non-immune visitor you are more likely to contract the illness than the residents, so you should make an extra effort to take anti-malaria prophylactics. Ask your doctor to explain their use and if necessary, start taking them before you actually arrive in Zimbabwe so that levels of the drug are built up in your system. Note that pregnant women should take more specific precautions.

Zimbabwean doctors currently recommend a combination of pyrimethamine-dapsone (Deltaprim, Maloprim, or Malasone) which are taken at the rate of one tablet a week. They recommend that you take the tablet weekly for a minimum of four weeks after returning home.

The College of Primary Care Physicians of Zimbabwe points out that no prophylactic is guaranteed 100 per cent effective for malaria prevention and therefore that the best means of prevention is to avoid the risk of being bitten by mosquitos through mechanical protection. This involves the use of repellant creams, lotions and sprays, mosquito nets and repellant coils and vapours.

Symptoms of malaria include a flu-like illness or a high fever with a splitting headache and, if malaria is advanced, discoloration of the urine.

Bilharzia

It is wise to assume that all slow-moving waters near habitation are infected with bilharzia.

You can assume that bilharzia is present in most rivers except for the fast-flowing rivers of the Eastern Highlands. It also exists in Lake Kariba, although some people say that it is safe to swim in the centre of the lake, always remembering that you still might be at risk from the crocodiles.

The parasite is present in water in which man, the principal host, has either urinated or defecated. Its intermediate host is a tiny water snail. The parasite, a worm-like fluke, enters the bloodstream and makes its way to the walls of the intestine or bladder, where it begins to lay eggs and multiply.

You are more likely to develop bilharzia if you have a cut in the skin through which the parasite can enter your system.

The most obvious indication of infection is a feeling of lassitude and malaise, possibly accompanied by a high temperature. These symptoms are likely to emerge up to six weeks after the initial infection. Once it has become well established, the more common symptoms are signs of blood in the stool and urine accompanied by possible abdominal pain.

If you have to swim in a river or dam, one way of avoiding infection is by rubbing yourself (and clothing) briskly with a towel on leaving the water. This is because the minute larvae die quickly when removed from water, and they are not likely to survive and penetrate the skin if rubbed with a towel.

Treatment consists of a single dose or short course of tablets which is usually effective as long as the correct dosage according to body weight is taken. If you do suspect that you may have bilharzia ask your doctor to do a stool and urine analysis when you get home. But remember that the eggs take between 30 and 40 days to develop so any tests done before this period has elapsed are likely to produce negative results.

Tickbite fever

If you walk in long grass in summer you are at risk of being bitten by a tiny tick which you will be unlikely to notice unless you are looking for it.

An infected bite usually has a yellow head with a small black central spot. The onset of the disease is usually rapid (seven to ten days) with symptoms such as severe aching of the bones, headaches, backaches, marked tiredness, fever and glands that become swollen and painful.

The illness is usually treated by a course of tetracycline. If you intend walking in the bush you should wear long trousers and socks and keep a lookout for any ticks that could be attached to your clothing.

A tick can be removed by smearing the part of it that is attached to the skin with Vaseline or any greasy substance. This will impede the tick's breathing and cause it to release its grip, making it easier to pull away when the grease is wiped off. Another means of forcing the tick to loosen its hold on the skin is to hold a lighted cigarette close to its body. If you just pull the tick out without using the methods outlined above, the tick's mouthparts are likely to be left behind, which can result in infection.

Snakes

Of the poisonous snakes, the most prevalent in Zimbabwe are the cobras and puff adders. Snakes in general are most likely to be seen in the months of September to May as they are less active and may hibernate during the colder months. Keep your eyes peeled when walking in the bush, especially for the very well camouflaged puff adders, which like lying in pathways. Walk carefully over logs or rocks for there may be a snake on the other side. Also wear closed shoes and long trousers. If your are confronted by an angry snake you should remain still until it has moved away as snakes are most likely to strike at moving objects.

If you are sleeping out of doors, try raising your bed at least 30 cm above the ground. A well tucked-in mosquito net or groundsheet that has been sewn in can also help. You should check the arms and legs of any clothing that has been left hanging up or lying around. Also check shoes before putting them on. Snakebite symptoms vary according to the type of snake, so instead of waiting for symptoms to develop take immediate action and get the victim to hospital or to the nearest doctor. Identification is vital for effective treatment so, if you can do so safely, try and kill the snake without crushing its head as mouthparts are used to identify snakes.

First ensure that the victim remains calm, as psychological shock can kill more easily and quickly than any venom. Keeping the victim calm will also ensure that venom is not rapidly circulated throughout the body. Give paracetamol and not aspirin for the treatment of pain.

Don't use antivenom without medical assistance. Don't suck out the venom or apply a tourniquet. Do not make any cuts at the site of the bite. Apply a pressure bandage over the bite and entire limb together with a splint to immobilise the limb and thus delay the spread of venom to the lymph glands. The bandage ideally should be made of crepe but torn clothing is equally useful. It should be as tight as for a sprained ankle.

Scorpions and spiders

These are most likely to be encountered when camping in the bush. Shake out clothes and empty shoes before putting them on. Be careful when picking up firewood and when touching loose bark on trees.

A sting/bite is unlikely to cause more than severe local pain but a few species can produce symptoms such as vomiting, diarrhoea and sweating. The more poisonous scorpion stings affect the heart muscle, causing a drop in blood pressure and possible heart failure. Contact a hospital immediately in case an adrenalin injection is needed to counteract a drop in blood pressure, which may occur in certain hypersensitive individuals. Otherwise, local anaesthetic and possibly a powerful analgesic can be used to treat the pain.

AIDS

AIDS is prevalent in Zimbabwe, but, as the health authorities have screened all donated blood for AIDS for several years and disposable needles are routinely used, there is no especial risk of contracting AIDS through medical treatment in Zimbabwe. Despite this and as in any other country that screens blood for AIDS, you would be wise to remember that there is a three-month "window" period where even if blood does contain the AIDS virus, it will not show up during analysis.

To be extra cautious if you are travelling overland, take your own supply of disposable needles and transfusion kits. Safe sex, i.e. with condoms, offers some protection against AIDS and venereal diseases.

The sun

The tropical sun can be vicious in summertime. Remember to acclimatise your skin to the sun by using graded sunscreens, which you should buy before you leave home as few suntan lotions are available in Zimbabwe.

Wear a wide-brimmed hat when outdoors and remember that clouds do not prevent the sun's rays from coming through.

Signs of heat exhaustion include feelings of nausea, illness and headaches. Increase your intake of water and possibly add a little salt to your diet.

Dental and optical matters

Have a dental check up before you leave home. Dentists can be located in the main towns in Zimbabwe and they are listed after doctors at the beginning of each town's listing in the telephone directory.

Likewise, bring a spare pair of specs if you wear glasses, and/or contact lenses and cleaning fluid.

First-aid kit

A fairly wide range of medicines can be purchased over the counter in pharmacies in the main towns. If you want to carry your own basic first-aid kit be sure to include the following:

tweezers
sticking plaster
lint
painkillers
antihistamine cream or tablets for stings and bites
a narrow and a wide bandage
safety pins
cotton wool
scissors
anti-diarrhoea medicine
antiseptic cream

Inoculations

Visitors from Western countries are not obliged to be inoculated against any diseases. However, if you will be "roughing it" check that your polio and tetanus vaccinations are in order. Always check with your travel agent when booking your flight whether any inoculations are mandatory. If coming from any areas where cholera and/or yellow fever are prevalent, you will have to be inoculated against these diseases.

SAFETY PRECAUTIONS

The bush

Do not try to feed animals even though they seem to be tame. This applies especially to the docile-looking but potentially murderous buffalo. Do not get out of your car to get a better photograph. Always obey national parks regulations.

If you come across an elephant, lion or any other dangerous wild animal, walk in the opposite direction if you can, but do not run as this might provoke it to chase you. Lions are at their most dangerous when mating, when very hungry or when attempting to protect their young. Never try to get between an elephant and its young. If walking on a river bank, try to avoid early morning or late afternoon when hippo might be traversing the area between the bank and water. These are the times when attacks are most likely.

Getting lost/breaking down

Carry lots of small change so that in an emergency you will be able to tip those who help you. If you plan to do a lot of motoring in Zimbabwe, it is worth paying the very reasonable fee to join the AAZ (Automobile Association of Zimbabwe – see page 111 for more details of their services).

Before entering a national park, check your spare wheel and see that access to it is not obscured by a heavy load. You need to be able to get to it in a hurry.

WHAT TO TAKE

General

Occasionally you will find that certain items are unobtainable. Zimbabwe's strict foreign exchange policy emphasises self-sufficiency and you will find mostly local brands on the shelves. Items which are usually hard to come by include watch, torch and camera batteries, binoculars, video camera and ordinary camera spares, film, electronic goods and spares, Western toys, disposable nappies and razor blades. If you're on a course of medication bring along an adequate supply.

Clothing

The quality and range of locally manufactured clothing is very good indeed and prices are competitive.

In summertime (September to April) you will need light clothing, but make provision for the odd cool, overcast day or windy night. During the rainy season it's wise to include a lightweight raincoat. If you are visiting the Eastern Highlands in summer, take along a light tracksuit for unexpected chilly weather. During the more transitional autumn and spring months and even in winter, wear clothing in layers that can be removed as temperatures rise and then replaced as they drop again.

It's worthwhile taking a hat and sunglasses to ward off glare and heat, especially if you are to spend a fair amount of time outdoors.

For game viewing remember that it is illegal for civilians to wear camouflage gear of any kind. Neutral or dull colours are far less likely to arouse the interest of game than are light and bright colours.

Zimbabweans are noted for their easygoing informality, though many hotels request that their male guests wear "smart casual" clothing, especially after 17:00. This means a short or long-sleeved shirt with collar and tie – shorts, jeans and sandals are unacceptable. If you plan to stay at the more upmarket hotels it would be wise to pack an evening shirt, tie and jacket.

Shoes

Visitors who will be doing a lot of walking should bring a pair or two of sturdy, solidly made shoes that have been broken in before the start of the trip. Do not walk barefoot in the bush. The lighter types of walking shoes and trainers are far more suited to Zimbabwe terrain than the European-style walking boot. Choose shoes that are quick to dry.

Locally manufactured shoes, especially the Bata brand, are very reasonably priced and come in a fairly wide range of styles.

Sporting equipment

Swimming – bring your own goggles and earplugs
Tennis – equipment can often be hired at courts
Riding – bring your own riding clothes
White water rafting – you just need a t-shirt, hat, sunglasses and shoes
Fishing – you can buy basic tackle in the bigger towns or hire it in the fishing resorts

Food and drink

Camping food is widely available, even in the smaller towns. For camping you'll need to take fresh food that lasts a while such as carrots, onions, cabbages, potatoes, oranges and lemons as well as dried fruit. Dried foodstuffs available in Zimbabwe include dried milk, crispbreads, packet soups, cheese, tinned meats and vegetables, rice and pasta.

Zimbabwe is noted for its beef, which is reasonably priced and of good quality. The braaivleis or barbecue is a very popular pastime in Zimbabwe and most campsites have built-in braaivleis areas. A tasty dried meat (biltong) is widely available, as is boerewors, a spicy sausage which is very popular in southern Africa. Bear in mind that one of the worst things that can happen to you is to smell other people's boerewors cooking over the fire at a campsite and not have any boerewors of your own to cook!

White bread is the most popular type and is available in most places. Brown and wholewheat bread are sold only in the main centres. As Zimbabwe is landlocked, fresh fish is limited to trout from the Eastern Highlands and bream from Lake Kariba. There is little tinned or fresh fish in supermarkets. A wide range of food is available in hotels and restaurants in the larger towns.

If you're a conservative wine drinker and prefer well-known international brands, then you will have to take your own wine. Zimbabwe makes its own palatable but not internationally rated wine. The same goes for local whiskies, brandies, cognac and gin. There is no large mineral water industry as the local tap water is very palatable and safe to drink. The Mazoe orange and lime squashes are especially good to drink.

Camping gear

You don't need to bring your own as it can all be hired in Zimbabwe, notably at Rooney's, 144 Seke Road, Harare, P. O Box 1351 Harare, Tel (14) 70–3515. They stock sleeping bags, gas cookers, chairs, tables, crockery, cutlery, glassware, barbecue equipment, baby kits and cooling equipment. Fereday & Sons fill gas cylinders, 72 Robert Mugabe Road, Harare, Tel (14) 70–4616.

Vehicles

See Chapter 5, Travelling inside Zimbabwe (page 101).

Photography

A variety of film is sold in Zimbabwe but bring your own to be on the safe side. There are a few 24-hour processing laboratories in Harare, Bulawayo and Victoria Falls. Quality and price are reasonable.

7. WHERE TO STAY

Good budget accommodation is easy to find in the larger towns, whereas in the more tourist oriented areas, prices tend to be higher.

For convenience this section focuses on hotel accommodation as distinct from national parks accommodation (see page 155). Prices have not been quoted although broad guidelines have been provided. In some cases, hotels are described as budget, medium and upmarket. Star ratings will also give the visitor an indication of quality although bear in mind that stars may be gained or lost after the publication of this guide. Listings are in alphabetical order by town rather than by region to help those who are not familiar with Zimbabwe's layout.

Also refer to safari listings.

ACCOMMODATION LISTED BY TOWN/RESORT

Beitbridge

**Beitbridge Hotel, P. O. Box 82 Beitbridge, Tel (186) 413. Rooms have bath or shower, phone, radio and TV, also swimming pool.

Peter's Motel, P. O. Box 21, Beitbridge, Tel (186) 309/321. All 39 rooms have bath, phone and air-conditioning. Full restaurant and swimming pool, TV lounge which also shows SATV.

Bubi/Bubye

Lion and Elephant Motel, Private Bag 9035, Masvingo, Tel Mwenezi (114–7) 01502. On Beitbridge/Masvingo Road, 77 km from Beitbridge. All 22 rooms have bath. Also tennis court, swimming pool and game park. The motel is well known for its tasty biltong.

Bulawayo

Budget

Municipal campsite and caravan park, within Centenary Park boundaries, on main road as you enter urban Bulawayo. Very close to all amenities and in lovely setting.

Youth Hostel, 52 Townsend Road, corner of Third Street, Tel (19) 7-6488. Two dormitories with eight beds in each. Self catering.

Medium

**Greys Inn, Robert Mugabe Way and Leopold Takawira Avenue, P. O. Box 527 Bulawayo. Tel (19) 6-0121. Centrally situated family hotel with 30 rooms all with phone and radio and private bath, swimming pool.

Hilltop Motel, Gwanda Road, Bulawayo, P. O. Box 2137 Bulawayo, Tel (19) 7-2493. 14 double chalets and four family chalets, plus restaurant and swimming pool.

**Hotel Rio, Old Esigodini (Essexvale) Road, past racecourse, 24 rooms have bath or shower, phone and radio. Swimming pool, children's playground.

**New Royal, George Silundika Street and Sixth Street, P. O. Box 1199 Bulawayo, Tel (19) 6-5764. Smallish, all rooms have bath, phone and radio. Full restaurant, TV available on request.

*Plaza Hotel, 14 Avenue, between Jason Moyo Avenue and Fife Street, P. O. Box 1521 Bulawayo, Tel (19) 6-4280. Rooms without baths are cheaper.

**Selborne Hotel, Leopold Takawira Avenue, P. O. Box 219 Bulawayo, Tel (19) 6-5741. All 30 rooms have bath, phone and radio. Some air-conditioned. Swimming pool. Very centrally situated opposite the City Hall.

YWCA Hostel, 35 Ninth Avenue, Tel (19) 6-0185. Rooms are more likely to be available in the holidays as it is popular with long-term students. Caters for both men and women.

Upmarket

***Bulawayo Holiday Inn, behind the Ascot Centre on your left as you enter the city on the Masvingo/Beitbridge road. Overlooking the Ascot racecourse, the hotel is not really within walking distance of the city. P. O. Box AC 88, Ascot, Bulawayo, Tel (19) 7-2464. All 151 rooms have bath, phone, radio, TV and air-conditioning. Swimming pool, saunas, tennis and squash. The hotel provides a courtesy transport service.

***Bulawayo Sun Hotel, corner of 10th Avenue and Josiah Tongogara Street, Tel (19) 6-0101, P. O. Box 654 Bulawayo. All 180 rooms have bath, phone, radio and TV plus air-conditioning. Situated in the heart of the commercial district and within walking distance of the city's shopping area. The hotel has two restaurants.

***Cresta Churchill**, corner of Matobo Road/Moffat Avenue, Hillside, drive about 6 km out of town towards Matobo National Park, P. O. Box 9140 Hillside, Tel (19) 4–1016. All 50 rooms in this mock-Tudor hotel have bath, phone, radio and TV. Restaurant, swimming pool.

Binga

(On south-west shore of Lake Kariba)

Binga Rest Camp, P. O. Box 9 Binga, Tel Binga (115) 244. Hot, spring-filled swimming pool. Rooms and chalets available as well as camping. Very reasonably priced. Meals available. 70 km from Mlibizi on un-tarred road.

Chimanimani

(Mountains, national park, eastern sector)

*****Chimanimani Hotel**, P. O. Box 5 Chimanimani, Tel (126) 511. 148 km from Mutare on tarmac road. Most of the 36 rooms have bath. Best rooms are those with a view of mountains, also more expensive. Swimming pool, bowls, tennis and walks to the Eland Sanctuary and Bridal Veil Falls are some of the hotel's attractions.

Chinhoyi

(115 km north-west of Harare)

Campsite, Chinhoyi Caves Recreational Park, 8 km north of the town. Adjacent to the Caves Motel, see below.

*****Caves Motel**, P. O. Box 230, Chinhoyi, Tel (167) 2340. Chalets with good restaurant in main building. Situated at turn off to recreational park.

****Orange Grove Motel and Caravan Park**, Independence Way, just outside Chinhoyi, P. O. Box 436, Chinhoyi, Tel (167) 2785. All rooms have bath and shower, phone and radio.

Chipinge

Chipinge Hotel, P. O. Box 27, Chipinge, Tel (127) 2226. Small hotel, good food.

Chiredzi

(Triangle/Hippo Valley area in the south-east, near Gonarezhou National Park)
*****Planter's Inn**, Marula Drive, P. O. Box 94, Chiredzi, Tel (131) 2281. All 26 rooms have either bath or shower, phone and air-conditioning. Also swimming pool.
****Tambuti Lodge Hotel**, P. O. Box 22 Chiredzi, Tel (127) 2575. Ten kilometres outside Chiredzi. Most of the 22 rooms have bath and shower. All have telephone and air-conditioning. Swimming pool, tennis court, good for birdwatchers. Three nearby golf courses. Fishing, game viewing at nearby hippo pools.

Chirundu

(Border post Zimbabwe/Zambia)
Albida Lodge, P. O. Box 9 Chirundu, or P. O. Box 193 Graniteside Harare, Tel Harare (14) 79–5686. Albida Lodge consists of a split-level tree house at Chirundu on the banks of the Zambezi River. Open all year round, camp activities include exceptional birdlife and game viewing. The small exclusive camp caters for six people.
Chirundu Valley Motel, P. O. Box 10, Chirundu, Tel Chirundu (163–7) 616.

Chivhu

(On the Masvingo/Harare Road)
*****Vic's Tavern**, P. O. Box 12 Chivhu, Tel (156) 2764. Eight of the 16 rooms in this one-star hotel have baths.

Deka

(To the north of Hwange town)
Deka Drum Fishing Resort, P. O. Box 2 Hwange, Tel Hwange (181) 5–0524. Just north of Hwange town take turn off and follow tarred road for 45 km. Chalets have bathroom and fridge plus linen. Camping as well. Very reasonable. Good base for fishermen. Restaurant, pool, petrol.

Dete

(Very near Hwange National Park)

*Gwaai River Hotel, P. O. Box 9, Gwayi, Tel Dete (118) 3400. Just off the Victoria Falls/Bulawayo Road about 38 km from Hwange National Park. All 23 rooms have bath or shower. Full restaurant facilities. Children's playground, horse riding, tennis. Good old fashioned value and an excellent alternative if you can't get accommodation in the park or at Hwange Safari Lodge.

Gonarezhou National Park

Chilojo Trails, privately run luxury camp near the famous red cliffs. Telephone Safari Interlink, Harare (14) 72-0527.

Chipimbi Safaris on Chipimbi River. Privately run, personal attention, ranch hunting arranged. Traditional rondavels. Phone Safari Interlink, Tel Harare (14) 72-0527.

Cresta Sandstone Safari Lodges, 175 Chinhoyi Street, P. O. Box 2833, Harare, Tel Harare (14) 70-3131. Both Induna and Kwali camps are situated on the border of Gonarezhou National Park.

Induna Lodge can accommodate a maximum of ten people in thatch and stone bungalows in an area surrounded by sandstone cliffs.

Kwali Camp comprises separate rondavels, with communal bathroom facilities which can accommodate a total of 20 people.

Great Zimbabwe

(About 28 km from Masvingo, near Lake Mutirikwi [formerly Lake Kyle]. See also entry under Masvingo)

Great Zimbabwe Hotel, Private Bag 9082, Masvingo, Tel (139) 2274. 41 rooms each with bath, telephone and radio, plus swimming pool, game tours and tours of Great Zimbabwe. Reasonably priced cottages for two. Near enough to the ruins to walk there. Also see entry under Lake Mutirikwi.

Gweru

(On Bulawayo/Harare Road)

Caravan park at the Gweru Sports Club on Robert Mugabe Way, P. O. Box 599, Gweru, Tel (154) 2929.

Chitukuko Hotel, corner of Third Street and Moffat Avenue, P. O. Box 1377, Gweru, Tel (154) 2861.

Fairmile Motel, Bulawayo Road, P. O. Box 1232, Gweru, Tel (154) 4144. 34 rooms with bath, phone, radio and TV, swimming pool, squash, full restaurant.

Midlands Hotel, Main Street, P. O. Box 276 Gweru, Tel (154) 2581. All 52 rooms have bath, radio, phone, TV and air-conditioning. Situated in city centre, just a few minutes from the major shopping area of this industrial city.

Harare

Budget

Coronation Park Campsite, 5 km south-east of city on Mutare Road. Ablution facilities.

Earlside Hotel, Fifth St/34 Selous Avenue, Tel (14) 72–1101. Dormitory accommodation available for backpackers at a discount rate. Separate, more expensive accommodation is also available. Swimming pool on premises.

Elizabeth Hotel, corner of Julius Nyerere Way and Robert Mugabe Road, Tel (14) 70–8591.

Fala Fala Lodge, 161 Union Avenue, Tel (14) 79–6606. The Fala Fala is aimed at the backpacking segment of the tourist market. Cooking facilities available.

Federal Hotel, 9 Harare Street, Tel (14) 70–6118.

Paw-Paw Lodge Guest House, 262 Herbert Chitepo Avenue, between 5th and 6th streets, Tel (14) 7–2401. Dormitory-type budget accommodation with bath and cooking facilities.

Queens Hotel, corner Robert Mugabe Road and Kaguvi Street, P. O. Box 520, Harare, Tel (14) 73–8977/8.

Toc-H, 163 Union Avenue and 148 Baines Avenue, Harare, Tel (14) 72–1566. The hostel is for men only. The price includes the cost of breakfast.

The Youth Hostel, 6 Josiah Chinamano Avenue, Harare, Tel (14) 79–6436. Caters for both men and women but with separate dormitories. Cooking facilities with crockery and cutlery supplied as well as hot water and showers. Set in an old house in a pleasant garden, the hostel is closed between 10:00 and 17:00.

Medium

The Ambassador, 88 Union Avenue, P. O. Box 872, Harare, Tel (14) 70–8121. All 82 rooms have bath, radio and TV and phone. Centrally situated.

The Bronte Hotel, 132 Baines Avenue, Harare, Tel (14) 79–6631. Most rooms have baths, TV sets are available for hire, all rooms have phone.

The Casamia Hotel, 120 Baines Avenue, Harare, Tel (14) 79–0066.

Cresta Lodge, adjacent to Mukuvisi woodlands, 6 km from Harare centre on Mutare Road. The recently opened lodge, which forms part of the Cresta chain, offers all rooms with bathroom and shower en suite plus radio and colour television. Some rooms are reserved for female guests only while one room is specifically designed to accommodate disabled guests. There is also a fully equipped business centre and restaurant.

***Cresta Oasis Hotel**, 124 Baker Avenue, P. O. Box 1541, Harare, Tel (14) 70–4217. A medium-sized hotel; all rooms have bath, phone, radio and TV. Swimming pool. Lockup parking facilities.

Courtney Hotel, Selous Avenue/Eighth Street, P. O. Box 3150 Harare, Tel (14) 70–6411. All rooms have bath, radio and telephone. A TV set can be provided if requested. Situated in the Avenues, near Greenwood Park.

The Executive Hotel, Fourth Street/Samora Machel Avenue, Tel (14) 79–2803. Centrally situated, all rooms with phone, bath, radio and TV.

Feathers Hotel, Sherwood Drive off Josiah Tongogara Avenue extension, Mabelreign, P. O. Box M200, Mabelreign, Tel (14) 2–8472. A small hotel. Eight kilometres from city centre, near 18–hole golf course.

George Hotel, King George Road, Avondale, Harare Tel (14) 3–6677. All 35 rooms have a phone, bath and radio. Some have television.

*Kamfinsa Park Hotel**, Arcturus Road, Greendale, Harare, P. O. Box GD80, Greendale, Harare, Tel (14) 4–8024. Twelve of the 20 rooms have bath, phone and radio.

The Kentucky Airport Hotel, St Patrick's Road, Hatfield, P. O. Box H63 Hatfield, Harare, Tel (14) 5–0655. Each of the 32 rooms has a bath and phone.

Machipisa Park Lane Hotel, 4495 Samora Machel Avenue East, P. O. Box HG 192, Tel (14) 70–7631. A smallish hotel, each room with bath, phone, TV and radio and air-conditioning. Private garden and swimming pool.

Red Fox Hotel, Greendale Avenue, off Samora Machel Avenue, Highlands, P. O. Box HG28 Highlands, Harare, Tel (14) 4–5466. All eight rooms have bath, phone and radio.
Selous Hotel, Sixth Street/Selous Avenue, Harare, Tel (14) 72–7940. All rooms have bath, phone and radio. TV sets available for hire.
*****Terreskane Hotel**, 102 Fife Avenue/Second Street, Harare, Tel (14) 70–7031. A small hotel near city centre. Can be noisy.

Upmarket

The top-of-the-range hotels expect visitors from abroad to pay in foreign currency while residents are permitted to use Zimbabwe dollars. You may also be given the option, in some cases, of showing that you have changed foreign currency equivalent to the hotel bill. Zambians, Malawians, Namibians, Botswanans and South Africans are not regarded as foreign and are permitted to pay the same tariff as locals, although the ruling may vary.

********The Cresta Jameson**, Samora Machel Avenue/Park Street, P. O. Box 2833 Harare, Tel (14) 79–4641. Phone, radio and TV in all rooms, plus private baths. Also swimming pool terrace and two restaurants. Lock-up parking.
********Harare Holiday Inn**, Samora Machel Avenue/Fifth Street, P. O. Box 7 Harare, Tel (14) 79–5611. All rooms have bath, radio, TV and air-conditioning. Swimming pool, security parking.
**********Meikles Hotel**, Jason Moyo Avenue, right in the centre of town overlooking Unity Square, P. O. Box 594, Harare, Tel (14) 79–5655/ 70–7721. Meikles has a long-standing reputation for excellence.
**********Monomotapa Hotel**, 54 Park Lane, Harare, P. O. Box 2445, Harare, Tel (14) 70–4501. Classy accommodation in a distinctive and very centrally situated landmark overlooking the city's main park.
**********The Sheraton**, Samora Machel Avenue, some distance from the city centre, Tel (14) 72–9771. Zimbabwe's largest hotel is rated five-star and certainly offers all the hotel facilities you could wish for.

Outside Harare

Hunyani Hills Hotel, situated at Lake Chivero (formerly Lake McIlwaine), 31 km from Harare. P. O. Box UUA404, Union Avenue, Harare, Tel Norton (162) 2236. A small hotel with only 13 rooms, each with bath and telephone, ideal for fishing enthusiasts.

Skyline Motel, 19 km from Harare on Simon Mazorodze/main Masvingo Road, P. O. Box 4150 Harare, Tel (14) 6-7588. Another small hotel that features river fishing as one of its attractions.

Cresta Pamuzinda Safari Lodge, 87 km from Harare, P. O. Box 2833 Harare, Tel (14) 70-3523 for central reservations. Luxury lodges in private game park. Activities include early morning and evening game walks, game drives, fishing and birdwatching. The lodge overlooks a flooded pan which attracts a wide array of game.

Hwange

(Town; 90 km north of Hwange National Park on Bulawayo/Victoria Falls road)

**Baobab Hotel, P. O. Box 120 Hwange, Tel. Hwange (181) 32-3493. Medium sized, 50 rooms with bath, phone and mostly air-conditioned. Swimming pool.

Hwange National Park

(Private accommodation)

Hwange Safari Lodge, P. O. Box DT 5792, Dete, Tel Dete (118) 393. All 105 rooms have bath and shower, phone, radio and air-conditioning. Pool, game activities, museum and aviary, shop. Superbly situated overlooking its own waterhole, which is very popular with animals at night and often during the day. A very upmarket alternative to staying at Main Camp. Its only disadvantage is that you have to drive some distance to the park.

Ivory Lodge offers ten en suite tree houses, built in indigenous hardwoods and furnished in ethnic style. The camp overlooks a waterhole.

Jijima Safari Camp, c/o Wild Horizons, P. O. Box 159, Victoria Falls, Tel (113) 4219/4349. On a private estate on the eastern boundary of Hwange National Park. It has large luxury tents under thatch with en suite facilities. The camp has its own swimming pool and overlooks a game watering pan. Walking and game drives are offered within the estate boundaries.

Makololo Tented Camp, Touch the Wild Ltd, Private Bag 5779, Dete, Tel Dete (118) 2105. Situated in the southerly part of the park, the tented camp overlooks a hippo pool. Accommodation is offered in large tents with flush toilets and hot showers. Foot and open Landrover safaris available. The camp is open all year, and a stay of three to five days is recommended.

Sable Valley Lodge, Touch the Wild Ltd, Private Bag 5779, Dete, Tel Dete (118) 2105. A chalet camp set in scenic surroundings on Dete vlei in Hwange offering 21 beds in thatched rondavels and the benefit of experienced guides to take you on safari.

Sikumi Tree Lodge, Private Bag 5779 Dete, Tel Dete (118) 2105. Near Hwange National Airport. Offers horse and foot safaris or you can choose to just watch game from your elevated tree house, of which there are 12 thatched, twin-bedded units set high in the branches of mangwe trees. The lodge has its own pool and electricity.

Makalolo Tented Camp, private luxurious camp offering accommodation in double tents in southern area of park. Telephone Safari Interlink, Harare (14) 72-0527.

Kwa Nemba, chalets in the bush. No children under 12. Safari Interlink, Harare, Tel (14) 72-0527.

Juliasdale

(About half an hour's drive to the west of Nyanga National Park)

***Brondesbury Park Hotel, P. O. Box 8070, Rusape, Tel Juliasdale (129) 343. Situated just off the main road. The 41 rooms have bath or shower and radio. Full restaurant, heated swimming pool, landing strip, billiards, 9-hole golf course, bowls, tennis. Half an hour's drive to the casino.

****Montclair Casino Hotel, P. O. Box 10, Juliasdale, Tel Juliasdale (129) 442. All 86 rooms of this Zimbabwe Sun hotel have bath, phone and radio. Golf, tennis, croquet, bowls, billiards, swimming pool, horse riding, casino and trout fishing.

Pine Tree Inn Hotel, P. O. Box 1 Juliasdale, Tel Juliasdale (129) 2-5916. Log fires in this warm, comfortable hotel with only 11 rooms, all with bath.

Kadoma

(On Bulawayo/Harare road)

***Kadoma Ranch Motel, P. O. Box 874 Kadoma, Tel Kadoma (168) 2106. 140 km south of Harare. Pool. Some rooms have baths and others have showers. All rooms have phone and radio. Good security.

*Speck's Hotel, Union Street P. O. Box 113, Kadoma, Tel Kadoma (168) 3302.

Kariba

(See also Lake Kariba entry)

Mopani Bay camping and caravan park, P. O. Box 130, Kariba, Tel Kariba (161) 2–2313. All ablution facilities, shop, on shores of lake just a couple of kilometres to the east of Kariba, access on Makuti road. Budget priced.

M.O.T.H. Cottages and Caravan Park, P. O. Box 67 Kariba, Tel Kariba (161) 2809. Campsites, or self-catering chalets and rooms. Very popular.

Caribbea Bay Resort and Casino, P. O. Box 120 Kariba, Tel Kariba (161) 2453/4. Sardinian-style hotel accommodation right on the lakeshore. Rooms or "casitas" ideal for families as they can each accommodate up to six people. Two swimming pools and casino. Caravan and camping facilities also offered.

**Cutty Sark Hotel, P. O. Box 80, Kariba, Tel (161) 2321 or central reservations office, Harare, P. O. Box 1490 Harare, Tel (14) 70–5081. All 65 rooms in this lakeshore hotel have air-conditioning, and ten of the units have attached porch rooms for children. Own swimming pool. A large bar-service cruise boat operates from the Cutty Sark twice a day. A full day cruise is also offered.

Kariba Breezes Hotel, P. O. Box 3 Kariba, Tel (161) 2433 or Harare, Tel (14) 79–0173. All 30 rooms have air-conditioning and bath. Also two swimming pools and private marina.

**Lakeview Inn, P. O. Box 100, Kariba, Tel (161) 2411/3. Good views. All 56 rooms have air-conditioning, phone and bath. Full restaurant facilities, swimming pool, Putt-Putt course and transport to the casino.

Most High Hotel, P. O. Box 88 Kariba, Tel Kariba (161) 2964. 15 double rooms and two family rooms, with air-conditioning and shower/bath. Superb views. Reasonably priced, run by evangelists who require that guests do not drink alcohol while on the premises. Smoking is not allowed inside the hotel.

Couples must also produce passports to prove they are married if they wish to share a room.

Tamarind Lodges, P. O. Box 1 Kariba, Tel (161) 2697. Recently established, Tamarind Lodges offer an alternative to hotel accommodation in their four- and six-bedded lodges. All lodges are semi-serviced and completely self-catering. Bedding, crockery and cutlery as well as cooking utensils, a fridge and a small two-plate cooking unit are provided. Bring your own towels, food, liquor and soap. The lodges are situated right near the entrance to Cutty Sark Hotel.

Zambezi Valley Hotel, Stand 643, Nyamhunga township, P. O. Box 105 Kariba, Tel (161) 2926. All 12 rooms have bath.

Karoi

(On Harare/Chirundu road)

**Karoi Hotel, P. O. Box 51 Karoi, Tel (164) 6317. Rooms with and without baths. All have a telephone and radio. Two family rooms.

Kwekwe

(On Bulawayo/Harare road)

Campsite and caravan park at Dutchman's Pool, about 10 km out of town and signposted from First Street.

***Golden Mile Motel, Gweru Road, P. O. Box 238, Kwekwe, Tel Kwekwe (155) 3711. Just a couple of kilometres outside the town on the Gweru/Bulawayo Road. Full restaurant facilities, swimming pool. All 24 rooms have bath, phone, radio and TV.

Sebakwe Hotel, P. O. Box 184 Kwekwe, Tel (155) 2981. 29 rooms, some with private bath. Full restaurant, children's playground.

**Shamwari Hotel, First Street, P. O. Box 659, Kwekwe, Tel (155) 2387.

Lake Kariba

(See also Kariba entry)

Buffalo Safaris and Zambezi Canoeing, P. O. Box 113, Kariba, Tel Kariba (161) 2827. Accommodation is in a tented camp, with game-viewing activities offered.

***Bumi Hills Safari Lodge, P. O. Box 41 Kariba, Tel (161) 2353. A three-star establishment, run by Zimbabwe Sun Hotels and situated about 50 km from Kariba on the southern shore on the edge of the Matusadona National Park. The lodge has 34 rooms, each with bath, fan, radio and phone and panoramic views of the lake. Access from Kariba is by boat or light aircraft. Activities include game viewing, boating and fishing.

Fothergill Island Safari Lodge, Private Bag 2081 Kariba, Tel (161) 2253. Open-style thatched lodges, swimming pool, restaurant and bar. Ten minutes from Kariba by plane. Safaris by foot, boat and vehicle.

Sanyati Lodge, at the mouth of the Sanyati Gorge, offers best tiger fishing on lake, exclusive accommodation in luxury chalets. Four luxury twin en suite thatched chalets and one cottage for four people. Has its own pool. Book through Safari Interlink, Tel Harare (14) 72–0527.

Spurwing Island, P. O. Box 101 Kariba, Tel (161) 2466, or contact Jet Tours in Harare, Tel (14) 79–2218/70–6432. The boat trip from Kariba takes approximately 40 minutes. A variety of accommodation is offered ranging from luxury tents under thatch to chalets with bath and shower. The complex also has a swimming pool and restaurant. Game viewing and fishing.

Tiger Bay Safari Camp, P. O. Box 102 Kariba or P. O. Box 2705, Harare, Tel (161) 2569. Sixteen attractive, open-style double lodges/thatched chalets with fans, showers, toilets and electricity. Situated up the Ume River, the furthest resort from Kariba. 90 minutes from Kariba by boat and 15 minutes by plane. Game drives, walking, boating and tiger fishing (bring your own tackle). Own swimming pool.

Macheke

(Just off the main Harare/Mutare A3 road about 60 km from Harare)

Macheke Hotel, P. O. Box 89 Macheke, Tel Macheke (179–8) 352.

Makuti

(On junction between Kariba and Chirundu/Harare A1. 72 km from Kariba, 359 km from Harare)

Clouds End Hotel, P. O. Box 3334 Harare, or P. O. Box 112 Karoi, Tel (163) 526. Superb views. Situated adjacent to Mana Pools National Park and Charara safari area. The hotel is popular with cross-border visitors en route from Lusaka to Harare and vice versa.

Mana Pools

Chikwenya Camp. Book through P. O. Box 825 Harare, Tel Harare (14) 70–5040. Luxury camp with guests brought in by plane, comprises eight lodges containing two beds each facing the river. The plane lands at the camp on certain days only, while road access is limited to the period between May and October, when the park is open. It is possible to reach the camp by boat along the river at other times of the year. Activities include game viewing by vehicle, boat or on foot with professional guides.

Ruckomechi Camp. Full board includes game activities but not transfers. Book through Safari Interlink/Safari Consultants, Tel Harare (14) 79–2218 or Jet Tours, P. O. Box 3622 Harare. Ten thatched chalets each containing two beds. Activities include canoeing, walks and game viewing by vehicle or boat. Same access arrangements as Chikwenya. Note that it is a tsetse area.

Marondera

(On main Harare/Mutare road A3, formerly Marandellas)

The Larkhill Barn, P. O. Box 23 Marondera, Tel (179) 34–1329. These are farm cottages offering either bed and breakfast or self-catering options. The Larkhill Barn is 60 km from Harare, and 6 km down the Wedza Finches Road.

*The Marondera Hotel, on main road, P. O. Box 6, Marondera, Tel (179) 4005.

Masvingo

**Chevron Hotel, P. O. Box 245 Masvingo, Tel (139) 2054/5. All 42 rooms have bath, radio and telephone. Full restaurant and swimming pool. It is the most central of the hotels situated on the main street, Robert Mugabe Street.

**Flamboyant Motel, P. O. Box 225 Masvingo, Tel (139) 2005. All 46 rooms have bath, phone and radio. Full restaurant and swimming pool. Situated just 2 km out of town on road to Great Zimbabwe.

Municipal campsite, 2 km out of town on the Mutare Road. Recommended, with showers.

Mazowe

(40 km north of Harare, hub of the citrus growing area)

Mazowe Hotel, P. O. Box 5, Tel (175) 2243. Small, only seven double rooms but also offering swimming pool, restaurant and mini-golf.

Mlibizi

(On the south-western shore of Lake Kariba, serves as the ferry terminal; prime fishing area)

Mlibizi Zambezi Resort, P. O. Box 660 Bulawayo. Tel Harare (14) 70–4501. Chalets, some of which are fully equipped and self-contained, camping site. Central restaurant, shop, petrol, swimming pool. Fishing boats, tackle and equipment for hire. Only resort on the lake in this area.

Mlibizi Safari Lodge, P. O. Box 298 Hwange or P. O. Box 6294 Harare. Tel Harare (14) 70–7072. Luxurious bungalows with four beds in each overlooking the Zambezi River. Restaurant and bar. Shop, squash, tennis, swimming, horse riding, safaris offered on foot, horseback, by canoe or vehicle. Transfers available from Victoria Falls or nearby airstrip.

Mutare

Balmoral Private Hotel, 'C' Avenue/Third Street, Mutare, Tel (120) 6–1435.

Campsite and Caravan Park, Christmas Pass, 6 km outside Mutare, Tel (120) 6–0020–11.

The Castle, Leopard Rock, Private Bag V7401 Mutare, Tel (120) 21–0320. Exclusive accommodation, full board for party of four, no children.

**Christmas Pass Hotel, P. O. Box 841 Mutare, Tel (120) 6–3818. All 17 rooms have bath, phone and radio. Swimming pool. Five kilometres outside Mutare towards Harare on the Christmas Pass.

City Centre Hotel, 62 Herbert Chitepo St/'D' Avenue, P. O. Box 653, Mutare, Tel (120) 6–2441. Rooms have baths. Tends to be noisy at night.

Cotswold Heights Chalets, P. O. Box 3101 Mutare, Tel (120) 6–2127. 25 km outside Mutare, very near Vumba Botanical Gardens. Two chalets.

Impala Arms Hotel, P. O. Box 524 Mutare, Tel (120) 6-0722. Nine kilometres outside Mutare on Vumba road. Superb views. Swimming pool. This hotel set in the foothills of the Vumba mountains consists of 20 rooms, eight with bath.

***Manica Hotel**, Aerodrome Road, P. O. Box 28 Mutare, Tel (120) 6-4431. All 104 rooms have bath, TV, radio, air-conditioning and phone. This Zimbabwe Sun hotel in the heart of Mutare also has a full restaurant.

White Horse Inn, P. O. Box 3193, Paulington, Mutare, Tel (120) 6-0325. On Vumba Road 17 km from Mutare. Superb situation in the Vumba mountains, ideal for walks. The inn consists of eight rooms and one cottage and has a pool.

Wise Owl Motel, P. O. Box 588 Mutare, Tel (120) 6-4643. On Christmas Pass. All 69 rooms have bath, phone and radio. Food recommended. Hotel also has swimming pool.

Lake Mutirikwi

(Old name Lake Kyle; very near to Great Zimbabwe. See also Masvingo entry.) Good base if Great Zimbabwe hotel is full; also good place for water sports when water level is up, check first though as level has been extremely low during the drought.

Kyle View Holiday Resort, Private Bag 9055, Masvingo, Tel (139) 22-3822. The resort comprises fully equipped chalets, a restaurant and shop, caravan and camping facilities and swimming pool on the shores of Lake Muturikwi, a short distance beyond the Great Zimbabwe turn off.

Muturikwi Lakeshore Cottages, P. O. Box 518, Masvingo, Tel (139) 2924-21. Fully equipped, attractively designed chalets to accommodate six. Along the same road as above, but just a bit further along. Also offers caravan and camping facilities.

Nyanga

(In the Eastern Highlands of Zimbabwe, 268 km from Harare on A3 – also see Juliasdale entry)

Nyanga Holiday Hotel, P. O. Box 19 Tel (129-8) 336. All 20 rooms have bath and radio. Also tennis. Cheapest option. In Nyanga town itself.

*Rhodes Nyanga Hotel, Private Bag 8024N, Rusape, Tel (129–8) 377. Formerly a residence of Cecil John Rhodes, set amidst pines, oaks and chestnuts with rose garden and museum.

Rusape

(At junction between Harare/Mutare and Nyanga roads)

Campsite and Caravan Park, 10 km from Rusape town at Rusape dam with full ablution facilities.

*Balfour Hotel, P. O. Box 95 Rusape, Tel (125) 2945. On Chimurenga Road. All 16 rooms have bath or shower.

Crocodile Motel, Harare/Mutare Road, P. O. Box 166. Tel (125) 2404. A small motel of only nine rooms, some with bath and some with shower, all with telephone and radio. The motel also has a swimming pool.

Troutbeck

(In Nyanga region, Eastern Highlands, easy access to Nyanga National Park)

***Troutbeck Inn, Private Bag 2000, Nyanga, Tel Nyanga (129–8) 305. All 75 rooms of this Zimbabwe Sun hotel built in 1947 by Major Herbert McIlwaine have bath, radio and phone. Permanent log fire in entrance hall. Situated nearly 2 000 m above sea level with surrounding mountains rising to nearly 2 300 m, it lies outside the Nyanga National Park to the north-east and can only be reached by driving through the park. It has its own trout-stocked, pine-fringed dam, as well as a very hilly and interesting golf course bordering a mountainous area. The weather tends to be cool and misty. There is lots to do here, including golf, riding, bowls, croquet, tennis, clay pigeon shooting, billiards and trout fishing. The food is good and the views excellent. The hotel offers a baby-sitting service, children's dining room and a playground. World's View, a panoramic and scenic viewpoint, is just 7 km from Troutbeck.

Victoria Falls

Budget

Victoria Falls Town Council Rest Camp and Caravan Park, P. O. Box 41 Victoria Falls, Tel (113) 4210. Offers accommodation in a campsite, chalets and hostels, right in the centre of town but some distance from the river. The 15-bed hostels are segregated by sex and offer bedding, cooking facilities and toilets but not pots or pans. The one and two-bedroomed chalets have cooking and washing facilities, electricity and communal ablution facilities. Two-bedroomed cottages have six beds with bathroom, shower and toilet. Tents are also available for hire and firewood can be purchased.

Fishing Camps – Kandahar, Sansimba, Mpala Jena. These camps are in wonderful settings on the river, within the Zambezi National Park, and offer really good fishing. Sansimba is 30 km upriver and Mpala Jena 17 km upriver.

Kandahar is open all year while Sansimba and Mpala Jena are open only during the period from 1 May to 31 October. Two boats per camp are allowed. Only single parties containing a maximum of ten will be admitted at a time. Facilities are basic with toilet and cold running water and a sleeping shelter. Best to bring your own cooking facilities such as gas.

Upmarket

***A'Zambezi River Lodge**, P. O. Box 130 Victoria Falls, Tel (113) 4561. All 87 rooms are air-conditioned with bath, radio and phone. Thatched, set outside town on the banks of the Zambezi, adjacent to the Zambezi National Park. Swimming pool; well situated for boat trips on the Zambezi and visits to the Zambezi National Park. Near to Elephant Hills Hotel, but the furthest hotel from Victoria Falls town. Hotel offers free transport for falls viewing, shopping or casino visits.

*****Elephant Hills Hotel**, P. O. Box 170 Victoria Falls, Tel (113) 4691 or contact Zimbabwe Sun Central Reservations, Tel Harare (14) 73-6644. Recently fully refurbished after lying derelict since its 1977 mortar attack during the war, and put back on the map by the delegates at the 1991 Commonwealth Heads of Government Conference who used it for their mid-conference break. Said to be the most luxurious hotel in southern Africa with a golf course to rival the world's best and most interesting.

***Ilala Lodge**, P. O. Box 18, Victoria Falls, Tel (113) 4737. This small (16 rooms) but fully functioning thatched hotel with its own swimming pool is opposite the Makasa Sun, on the main road and within easy walking distance of the Falls, just 1 km away. Opened in 1991.

Imbabala Safari Camp, P. O. Box 159 Victoria Falls, Tel (113) 4219. A-frame chalets in the heart of elephant country on the Zambezi River upstream from Victoria Falls and close to the Botswana border. Consists of eight en suite lodges with pool. Gas lamps are used. No children allowed. The camp has a motorised pontoon for river game viewing and cruises. Game drives are also offered.

****Makasa Sun Hotel and Casino**, P. O. Box 90, Victoria Falls, Tel (113) 4275. A Zimbabwe Sun hotel with casino. The closest hotel to the Victoria Falls, just ten minutes' walk away, depending on the heat. Each of the 110 rooms has a bath, shower, phone, radio and air-conditioning. Children's playground, tennis courts, swimming pool, game enclosure. Family rooms are available.

Masuie Lodge – still under construction at time of writing.

***Rainbow Hotel**, P. O. Box 150 Victoria Falls, Tel (113) 4585. All 46 rooms have bathroom en suite plus telephone and air-conditioning. Ten minute walk from falls.

Sprayview Hotel, P. O. Box 70, Victoria Falls, Tel (113) 4344. Self-contained chalets, ideal for families. On the outskirts of town. 49 rooms with bath/shower, phone, radio and air-conditioning, as well as Olympic-sized pool, full restaurant facilities, children's playground, baby-sitting service and shop.

****Victoria Falls Hotel**, P. O. Box 10 Victoria Falls, Tel (113) 4203. Each of the 137 rooms of this gracious and historic hotel has a bath and shower, phone, radio and air-conditioning. Swimming, tennis and Putt-putt facilities. Superbly situated, with good view of railway bridge, but not the actual falls. Very popular, expensive and with an interesting past. It hosts the African Dance Spectacular nightly. The hotel boasts its own chapel in the court extension in which a number of guests have been married and then spent their honeymoon in the hotel. Up to 30 guests can be accommodated in the chapel.

Victoria Falls Lodge, still under construction at time of writing.

Westwood Lodge, P. O. Box 185 Victoria Falls, Tel (113) 4571. Situated on the banks of the Zambezi, this luxury camp offers an all-inclusive rate. It is a 45-minute drive from Victoria Falls and offers excellent fishing, canoeing, game-viewing. Accommodation consists of 12 bedrooms in thatched/stone chalets.

Vumba

(Botanical Gardens; just outside Mutare)

Campsite, clean, hot water, superb views, nearby shop.

Leopard Rock Hotel was closed during and after the war. Now recently reopened with superb golf course and casino.

NATIONAL PARKS ACCOMMODATION

Various types of accommodation are available in the national parks. You can choose from over 150 chalets, lodges and cottages at parks throughout Zimbabwe, all of which are clean and reasonably priced. Basics such as crockery, cutlery, bedding and hard furniture are provided while ablutions range from shared facilities to your own private bathroom. Lighting is by paraffin, gas or electricity while cooking facilities range from braais (barbecues) to gas or electric stoves.

When booking accommodation you can state which type of accommodation you would prefer but this may not be guaranteed. Accommodation is open to the reserved guest from 14:00 on the day of arrival to 10:00 on the day of departure.

To be sure of getting accommodation when you want it, book up to six months in advance at:

The Central Booking Office, The Travel Centre, 93B Jason Moyo Avenue, Harare, Tel. (14) 70–6077. The offices are open from Monday to Friday from 07:45 to 16:15. You could also book by post by writing to **The Central Booking Office**, P. O. Box 8151, Causeway, Harare.

School holidays and weekends are the most congested, although even if you haven't booked in advance, you could still risk turning up or phoning just before arriving, although Nyanga is likely to be an exception. In such cases you may be required to wait until 17:30, the cut-off point for guests who have booked and not arrived and when their rooms are given to visitors who have arrived without booking. This might be inconvenient in some cases if the guests do arrive and you haven't made alternative accommodation plans.

Chimanimani National Park

Situated at the foot of the mountains 21 km from Chimanimani town. Camping is allowed anywhere in the park as well as at Mutekeswane, which is the park base camp and which offers ablution facilities. Bring all your own provisions. There is also a mountain hut which is a two-hour hike from Mutekeswane. It has a gas cooker, basic beds and washing facilities.

Chizarira National Park

To the south of Lake Kariba and inland.

Offers three exclusive camps, which means that only one party at a time can use the camp. The best of these is Kasiwi, 6 km from park offices, which comprises thatched shelters on stilts. It has hot and cold water and cooking facilities and toilet and shower. Busi Bush Camp, which is 35 km from the offices, has only sleeping shelters. Mabolo Bush Camp is on Mucheni River, 6 km from the park offices. Bring your own tent; water is available from a spring. The camp is the least developed of the three.

Gonarezhou National Park

(See page 140 for privately owned accommodation)

Swimuwimi rest camp offers three five-bed thatched chalets with closed verandahs and two three-bedded chalets with open verandahs. It is fully equipped except for cutlery and crockery. There is a central ablution block.

Mbalauta camping and caravan site has a central ablution block with hot and cold water. Washing and outside cooking facilities are available.

Hwange National Park

Offers chalets, self-catering lodges and campsites as well as the option of camping in picnic areas. The park has three major camps: Main, Robins and Sinamatella.

Main Camp, Tel Dete (118) 371 or contact the warden, Main Camp, Private Bag DT 5776, Dete. Camping, chalets with barbecue facilities (but no crockery or cutlery), wash basin and communal ablution facilities; one and two-bedroomed cottages with internal bathroom and verandah, communal cooking facilities with electric hotplates; and lodges with electric cooking facilities and fridges and crockery and cutlery. There is also a bar, full restaurant and well-stocked shop. Petrol and diesel are available.

Sinamatella Camp, open all year round, Tel Hwange (181) 4–4255. Has huts/lodges with gas lighting, electric cookers. Cottages and chalets do not have crockery and cutlery, but do have electrical cooking facilities. There is a campsite, a store, restaurant and petrol.

Bumbusi Exclusive Camp, some 24 km north-west of Sinamatella with four A–frame units, each with two beds. There is also a cottage with two beds and a central lounge area with an extra two beds. A maximum of 12 can be accommodated. Fully equipped kitchen with gas cooker and fridge and central ablution block. Open all year round. You will need four-wheel drive during the rains to reach Bumbusi.

Lukosi Camp in Sinamatella area, an exclusive camp accommodating a maximum of 12 from November to April.

Nantwich, Robins and Deka camps (Tel Hwange (181) 7–0220, or write to the Warden, Robins Camp, Private Bag WK 5936, Hwange) have game viewing roads which are usually closed from 1 November to 30 April although accommodation remains open. Nantwich and Robins in the north-west corner of the park have an 11 km stretch of gravel road separating them.

Deka is situated 25 km to the west of Robins Camp. The camp's road is suitable for four-wheel drive vehicles only and is normally closed during the rainy season. It offers two family units with two bedrooms (three beds each) in each with bathroom and toilet. Another fully serviced unit has a dining room, lounge, kitchen with stove and fridge. A maximum of 12 people can be accommodated.

Robins Camp has chalets only with outside cooking, communal ablution blocks and no crockery or cutlery. There is limited lighting from dusk till 22:00. There is also a camping and caravan site.

At *Nantwich*, the lodges are fully self-contained with full 24–hour battery-generated electricity, crockery and cutlery. A store supplying basics and petrol and diesel is available.

Lake Chivero

(Formerly Lake McIlwaine; just south of Harare)

The national parks section offers chalets and lodges.

Lake Mutirikwi Recreational Park

(Formerly Lake Kyle Recreational Park; very near to Great Zimbabwe and also to Masvingo, see both those entries as well)

The national parks campsite at Sikato Bay is just 5 km from Great Zimbabwe. There are nine campsites with ablution and cooking facilities. There are also nine fully equipped lodges, six of which have one bedroom (three beds) while three have two bedrooms (five beds).

Lake Kyle: See Lake Mutirikwi

Mana Pools National Park

To the north-west of Harare. Two lodges, each sleeping eight, and very reasonably priced, on the banks of the Zambezi. The lodges can be booked six months in advance and are very popular.

Of the campsites the largest, Nyamepi, is near headquarters office, while Mucheni, Nkupe, Old Tree Lodge and Vundu have huts and hot and cold running water. All are situated on the river. See also under Mana Pools private accommodation. Remember this is a tsetse area.

Matobo National Park

To the south of Bulawayo. You can choose to camp at Maleme Dam caravan and camp site with hot and cold ablution facilities. If you wish to take a caravan, bear in mind that the site has a very steep access road.

At Mtshele Dam there is a campsite with ablution block. All drinking water must be boiled.

Toghwana Dam campsite has an ablution block with hot and cold water. Drinking water must be boiled.

One- and two-roomed chalets, ablution blocks and outside cooking facilities. One-roomed chalets have electric cooker but no crockery or cutlery. Lodges are fully equipped and with electricity. Just bring food.

Two luxury lodges, Fish Eagle and Black Eagle, are in a beautiful setting near Maleme Dam with lovely views. Each lodge contains five beds and is very reasonably priced.

Matusadona National Park

To the immediate south of Lake Kariba. Accommodation comprises national parks campsites. You need to bring all your own supplies. There is an airstrip at Tashinga. Camping equipment is available for hire.

At Sanyati there are three exclusive camps available for groups up to 12 staying for a minimum of six days, usually Monday to Sunday. The charge is for the entire camp, which consists of two units each with two bedrooms containing three beds each (total six beds in one unit), bathroom, toilet and bath. Each dining unit has a kitchen, fridge and solar-powered lighting. Other lighting is by gas and there is basic furniture, crockery and cutlery. Bring all your own provisions and note that there are no professional guides to assist you. Your party must be self-reliant for the duration of your stay.

At Tashinga campsite you can hire camping equipment and there are ablution facilities with hot and cold water, and barbecue facilities.

Nyanga National Park

Campers are well catered for with a number of campsites around the park. Bring your own food supplies. The park shop sells basics but no fresh food.

Rhodes Dam and Udu Dam are near the main entrance and park headquarters, while Mare Dam is further on. The lodges have one and two bedrooms to accommodate up to eight people. They are serviced.

Rhodes Dam Lodge is near to the hotel, shop and road, and overlooks a small dam. Well sited for walking.

Mare Dam, in a more isolated area of the park, will appeal to riders as stables are nearby and also to mountain climbers as it is closest to Mount Nyangani.

Udu Dam features thatched lodges set in indigenous vegetation as opposed to the exotic pines found in many parts of the park.

Zambezi National Park

This park has some 20 beautifully situated lodges, fully self-contained and right on the river. You can watch game wander freely down to the water and graze on your doorstep. Beware the monkeys, who will steal any food left unguarded. Each lodge is built to accommodate a maximum of six in two bedrooms, with a bathroom with bath and shower and electric kitchen.

The lodges are at the entrance to the park, just 6 km out of town. As they are understandably very popular, and a good budget alternative to the pricier Victoria Falls hotels, it is worthwhile to book in advance.

There is no shop nearby although you would be able to get most provisions from Victoria Falls town.

RESTAURANTS IN THE MAIN CENTRES

Bear in mind that considering the variable nature of the restaurant trade, some of the restaurants listed below may have closed down, and new ones may have opened which are not listed here.

Harare

Acropolis	Tel 3-9181. Avondale Shops, King George Road. Greek. No bookings. Takeaway also.
Alexander's	Tel 70-0340. 7 Livingstone Avenue. Supposedly the best in town.
Aphrodite Taverna	Tel 3-5500/3-9135. Strathaven Shopping Centre, Harare. Mediterranean food. Lunch and dinner.
Bamboo Inn	Tel 70-5457. 81 Robert Mugabe Road, (opposite 1st street) Harare, Chinese. Lunch/supper.
The Beefeater	Tel 30-2730. Strathaven Galleries, Suffolk Road. International cuisine.
Bellavista	Tel 88-2310. Greystone Park Shopping Centre, Greystone Park. Many vegetarian dishes. Booking not necessary.
The Bombay Duck	7 Central Avenue (between 2nd and 3rd Streets), Harare. Curries and takeaways.
Brazita Coffee House	Tel 79-2229. Southampton Parkade, Union Avenue. Open during day.

The Carvery	Tel 70–2484. Fife Avenue Mall, cnr Fife Avenue and 6th Street. Meat features strongly. Buffet as well as à la carte. Lunch and dinner.
The Cellar	Tel 2–3949. Marimba Shopping Centre, Samora Machel Avenue West. French cuisine.
Clovagalix	Tel 72–1850. Fife Avenue Shopping Centre. Good garlic steaks/seafood. Lunch and dinner. No bookings.
Coimbra	Tel 70–0234. 61 Selous Avenue. Portuguese. Peri-peri chicken recommended. No bookings.
Copacabana	Tel 73–6727. Cnr Chinhoyi St/Speke Avenue. Portuguese.
Demis	Tel 72–3308. Corner Speke Avenue/Leopold Takawira Street. Seafood/Greek food. Lunch and dinner.
L'Escargot	Tel 70–6411. Courtney Hotel, corner Selous Avenue and 8th Street. French. Booking necessary.
Europa	Tel 72–1367. 5 Throgmorton House, Samora Machel Avenue. Open all day.
Eros Tavern	Tel 70–8452. Kine Centre, Julius Nyerere Way. Italian. Near cinemas.
The Front Page	Tel 70–3201. Linquenda House, 58 Baker Avenue. International cuisine.
Guido's	Tel 72–3349. Montagu Shopping Centre, Josiah Chinamano Avenue. Italian. No booking. Supper only. Queuing.
Harvest Garden	Tel 72–9771. Sheraton Hotel. Buffet and salad selection.
Holly's Kitchen and Wine Bar	Tel 30–2730. Strathaven Shopping Centre. Lunch/supper.
Homegrown Restaurant	Tel 70–3545. Reliance House. Corner Speke/Leopold Takawira Street, Harare. Mostly vegetarian. Booking not necessary.
The Howff	Tel 4–8020. Chisipite Shopping Centre, Hindhead Avenue, Chisipite. Scottish food. Pub grub.

162 Zimbabwe

Italian Bakery	Tel 3-9732. Avondale Shops, 144 King George Road, Avondale. Stays open late.
Le Francais	Tel 30-2706. 7 Arts Complex, Avondale. French cuisine.
The Lido	Tel 73-0730. 51 Union Avenue. Near to cinemas. Good waffles. No booking.
Manchurian	Tel 3-6166. Belgravia Shopping Centre, 2nd Street extension. Mongolian food/stir fry. Booking. Supper only.
Mandarin	Tel 72-6277. 1st Floor, Ivory House, Robert Mugabe Way. Chinese. No booking. Lunch and dinner.
Pino's	Tel 79-2303. 73 Union Avenue (opposite New Parkade) Harare. Italian and seafood. Lunch/supper. Book in advance.
La Pizza	Tel 72-5535. 48 Angwa Street. Italian. Unlicensed.
Ramambo Lodge	Tel 79-2029. 1st Floor, BB House, corner Samora Machel Avenue/Leopold Takawira Street. Ethnic and game dishes. Lunch and dinner.
Sandros	Tel 79-2460. 50 Union Avenue Harare. Mediterranean cuisine. Open lunch/dinner. Near cinemas (Kine 1 and 2).
Shezan	Tel 70-0207. 88 Robert Mugabe Road, opposite Meikles department store. Pakistani cuisine. Open lunch and dinner.
Sitar Restaurant	Tel 72-9132. 39A Newlands Shopping Centre, Enterprise Road, Harare. Indian cuisine and takeaways.
Spagos	Tel 79-0565. Russell Hotel, 116 Baines Avenue. Pasta dishes.
Squabbles	Tel 73-2940. Newlands Shopping Centre, Victoria Drive, Highlands. International.
Tacos	Tel 70-0377. Lintas House, 46 Union Avenue. Mexican, Greek cuisine and steaks. No booking.

Tobacco Barn	Tel 3-5971. Mount Pleasant Shopping Centre. International.
Two Flights Up	Tel 72-7694. Cuthberts Building, First Street Mall, Harare. Snacks and full meals. Breakfast and lunch only. No booking.
Upper Crust Coffee Shop	Tel 70-3710. Batanai Mall, Batanai gardens. Health food. Open during day only.
Wombles	Tel 88-2747. Ballantyne Park Shopping Centre, Ballantyne Park. Steaks.
Your Place Restaurant	Tel 70-4355. 99 Robert Mugabe Road. International cuisine.

Bulawayo

Bon Journee	Tel 6-4839. 105 Robert Mugabe Way. Grills.
Buffalo Bill's	Tel 6-5741. Selborne Hotel, Leopold Takawira Avenue. Steakhouse.
Capri	Tel 6-8639. George Silunduka St/11th Avenue. Italian food.
Golden Spur	Tel 7-0318. 85 Robert Mugabe Way. Steakhouse.
La Gondola	Tel 6-2986. corner Robert Mugabe Way/10th Avenue. Italian restaurant.
Granada	Tel 7-0716/66-8464. 1st Floor, Parkade Centre, Fife Street/9th Avenue. Spanish food.
The Grass Hut	Tel 6-3180. 88 Fife Street. Good breakfasts and snack menu.
Haddon & Sly	Tel 6-5511. Fife St/8th Avenue. Open during day only. English teas and lunches.
Jade Moon	Tel 7-6086. Josiah Tongogara Street/10th Avenue. Opposite Bulawayo Sun Hotel. Chinese/vegetarian.
The Loft	Tel 6-9265. Corner 14th Avenue/Fife Street. Steaks/seafood.
Maison Nic	Tel 6-1884. Warnborough Mansions, Main St/4th Avenue Bulawayo. French cuisine.

New Orleans	Tel 4-3176. Between Leander Avenue and Cecil Avenue, off Banff Road, Hillside. Cajun/Dixie cuisine.
The Oasis	Tel 6-9662. Josiah Tongogara St/9th Avenue. Fast food.
Pagoda	Tel 7-2464. Ascot Centre, Milnerton Drive. Mongolian.
Peking	Tel 6-0646/6-6935. Treger House, Jason Moyo Street. Chinese food. Lunch and dinner.
Pizzaghetti	Tel 7-7460. George Silundika Avenue. Takeaways, chicken and pizza.
Top of the Sun	Tel 6-0101. Bulawayo Sun Hotel. Wilson Street. International cuisine. Booking advisable. Secure parking.

Mutare

Stax Steak House	Opposite Manica Hotel. Only restaurant open at night.

8. MISCELLANEOUS INFORMATION

Security

Not long ago guerrilla activity was rife in Zimbabwe and tourism was a risky business. But the country is at peace once again and tourism is on the increase. Incidents of violence are rare and the Zimbabweans seem intent on rebuilding and developing their country.

Unlike many more developed countries, Zimbabwe is prone to petty rather than violent crime. At most, when in the cities you should watch your pocket and do not leave any valuables lying around. And wherever you are, make sure your car is secure. You will find the police helpful and courteous as long as you don't antagonise them.

Banks

Four groups operate in Zimbabwe – Barclays, Standard Chartered, Zimbank and Grindlays. Banks are usually open from 08:30 to 14:00 Monday to Friday with an early closing on Wednesday, when doors are shut at midday. On Saturday business hours are from 08:30 to 11:00.

After hours it is sometimes possible to change money at hotels, particularly if you are a resident of that hotel, but don't depend on it. Strangely enough, hotel exchange rates seem in some places to be more favourable than the bank rate.

If asked by someone to change money on the black market, be aware that he might be a member of the fraud squad. In view of the country's tight foreign exchange situation, Zimbabwe's fiscal police are always on the lookout for defaulters.

Facilities countrywide

The following is a general breakdown of the type of facilities to be found in different areas:

Category 1

Bulawayo, Gweru, Harare, Masvingo, Mutare.

You can obtain everything you would expect to find in a modern town, e.g. banks, pharmacies, hairdressers, supermarkets, medical facilities and accommodation.

Category 2

Bindura, Chinhoyi, Chipinge, Chiredzi, Gwanda, Hwange, Kadoma, Kariba, Karoi, Kwekwe, Marondera, Victoria Falls, Zvishavane.

Supermarkets, accommodation, police, basic medical services.

Category 3

Banket, Beitbridge, Buffalo Range, Chegutu, Chivhu, Chimanimani, Mbalabala, Mutoroshanga, Mutoko, Mvurwi, Nyanga, Rusape, Shamva, Shurugwi, Triangle.

These are large villages where less specialised items are available in the shops, but where you can still get accommodation, fuel, pharmaceutical supplies, medical attention, police and supermarkets.

Category 4

Beatrice, Binga, Cashel, Chatsworth, Chirundu, Dete, Headlands, Guruve, Kamativi, Macheke, Makuti, Mlibizi, Msuna, Mvuma, Mwenezi, Penhalonga.

Only very basic goods can be found here and sometimes they may be out of stock, particularly of fuel. However, you can still find accommodation, medical facilities, police, and car repairs.

Business hours

Shops in the larger centres are usually open from 08:00 or 08:30 to 17:00 during the week and until 12:00 or 13:00 on Saturdays. Shops in rural areas may close for lunch between 13:00 and 14:00. Post offices open from 08:30 to 16:30 from Monday to Friday and close at 11:00 on Saturday. Selected pharmacies offer 24 hour service in the larger centres.

Shopping

Department stores and boutiques are generally open between 08:30 to 17:00 Monday to Friday, and on Saturday from 08:30 to 12:30. An 18 per cent general sales tax (at the time of writing) is imposed on all commodities including airline tickets but excluding unprocessed foodstuffs. Tax is included in prices quoted.

Most things are available in the main centres, but notable exceptions include: some sports equipment, a wide range of imported liquor, some batteries (especially watch and camera batteries); disposable nappies;

some baby formulas; more sophisticated photographic supplies and decent razor blades. As you penetrate the rural areas there is less variety and more emphasis on the basic commodities. (See Facilities countrywide, page 165.)

Government ministries and departments

Ministry/department	Address	Telephone
Civil Aviation	P/Bag 7716 Causeway Harare	(14) 79-2631
Community and Cooperative Development	P/Bag 7735 Causeway Harare	(14) 79-2351
Customs and Excise	P. O. Box 8015 Causeway Harare	(14) 79-0801
Education	P. O. Box 8022 Causeway Harare	(14) 73-4067
Energy, Water Resources and Development	P/Bag 7758 Causeway Harare	(14) 70-7861
Defence	P/Bag 7713 Causeway Harare	(14) 70-0155
Finance, Economic Planning and Development	P/Bag 7705 Causeway Harare	(14) 79-4571
Foreign Affairs	P. O. Box 4240 Harare	(14) 79-4681
Health	P. O. Box 8204 Causeway Harare	(14) 73-0011
Home Affairs	P/Bag 505D Harare	(14) 72-3653
Immigration Control	P/Bag 505D Harare	(14) 72-3653
Industry and Commerce	P/Bag 7708 Causeway Harare	(14) 70-2731
Information, Posts and Telecommunications	P. O. Box 8232 Causeway Harare	(14) 70-3891
Justice, Legal and Parliamentary Affairs	P/Bag 7704 Causeway Harare	(14) 79-0902
Labour, Manpower, Planning and Social Welfare	P/Bag 7707 Causeway Harare	(14) 79-0871
Land, Agriculture and Rural Resettlement	P/Bag 7701 Causeway Harare	(14) 70-6081

Ministry/department	Address	Telephone
National Supplies	P/Bag 7742 Causeway Harare	(14) 70–6446
National Museums and Monuments	P. O. Box 8540 Causeway Harare	(14) 79–0044
National Parks and Wildlife Management	P. O. Box 8365 Causeway Harare	(14) 70–7624
Natural Resources	P. O. Box 8070 Causeway Harare	(14) 79–4455
Office of the President and Cabinet	P/Bag 7700 Causeway Harare	(14) 70–7091
Police	P. O. Box 8028 Causeway Harare	(14) 73–3033
Transport	P. O. Box 8109 Causeway Harare	(14) 70–7121
Tourism	P. O. Box 8052 Causeway Harare	(14) 70–6511
Veterinary Services	P/Bag 7701 Causeway Harare	(14) 70–6081

Language and customs

Zimbabweans of all races are generally friendly and courteous, particularly in the rural areas.

The three main and official languages are Shona (spoken by 70 per cent of the population, mainly in the north and east); Sindebele (spoken by 15 per cent, mainly in the west and south) and English, which is the most widely understood language.

It is very unlikely that you may have to refer to the table below in order to make yourself understood, as most people speak or understand English. However, any attempt to converse with people in their mother tongue will always be appreciated, even though it may raise a giggle.

Sindebele is derived from Zulu and both languages are mutually understandable while Shona, subdivided into six main dialects, is more specific to the region.

As far as religion is concerned, Catholicism has the largest membership of the organised churches, although traditional religions are still strong and indigenous forms of Christianity have attracted fairly large numbers.

Useful words and phrases

English	Shona	Sindebele
Hello (sing)	Mhoro	Sawubona
Hello (plural)	Mhoroi	Salibonani
Hello (reply)	Ehoi	Yebo
How are you?	Makadii zvenyu	linjani/kunjani
good/very well	ndiripo zvangu	skhona/ ngiyaphila
bad	handisi kunzwa zvakanaka	angiphilanga kuhle
thank you	ndatenda/mazvita	ngiyabonga/siyabonga kakulu
please	ndapota	uxolo
goodbye	chisarai zvakanaka	lisale sesihamba lisala kuhle
welcome	titamberei	siyaalemukela
danger	ngozi	mingozi
friend	shamwari	mngane/umngane
sorry	ndine urombo	uxolo
excuse me	pamusoroi	uxolo/ngixolela
good morning	mangwanani	livuke njani
good afternoon	masikati	litshonile
good evening	manheru	litshone njani
yes	ehe	yebo
no	aiwa	hayi
how much?	imarii?	yimalini?
meat	nyama	inyama
fish	hove	inhlanzi
eggs	mazai	amaganda
potatoes	matapiri	amagwili
fruit	muchero/michero	izithelo
water	mvura	amanzi
vegetables	muriwo	umbhida, imbhida
beer	doro/whawha	utshwala
milk	mukaka	ucago
Mr/Sir	changamire	umnimzana
Madam	mudzimai	inkosikazi
What is your name?	Unonzi ani zita rako?	Ibizo lakho ngubani?

Petrol, diesel and air supplies

See section on Travelling inside Zimbabwe (page 104).

Public and school holidays

1 January	New Year's Day
Easter (variable)	Good Friday to Easter Monday
18 April	Independence Day
1 May	Workers Day
25/26 May	Africa Day
11/12 August	Heroes' Day
25/26 December	Christmas/Boxing Day

School holidays (slightly variable)

Early December to mid-January

Mid-April to mid-May

Early August to mid-September

Foodstuffs

Black Zimbabweans eat the staple maize or mealie-meal porridge (sadza) together with a relish which can be based on a vegetable or meat stew. Otherwise, English-style cooking predominates and a wide choice of ethnic and Western food is available in the larger centres.

Try the local Zimbabwean beef, which is comparatively cheap and of good quality. Be prepared for giant servings, for Zimbabweans are reputed to have big appetites.

As the country is landlocked, fish is limited to local trout and Kariba bream and kapenta, a very small fish which is dried and identifiable by its strong taste. Kapenta is mainly eaten by the locals. Tinned foodstuffs are all locally produced and include a fairly wide variety of jams, marmalades, fruits, vegetables and beef products. Different fruits and vegetables are in season at different times throughout the year.

Drinks

As tight foreign exchange restrictions exist, the importation of liquor is limited and consequently much effort has been put into establishing self-sufficiency in the field of liquor production.

Beer can almost be classed as the Zimbabwean staple drink. It is available as chibuku, a thick, porridge-like sorghum brew drunk mostly by black Zimbabweans, and a small range of lagers and pilsener, usually drunk ice-cold.

Zimbabwe also produces an acceptable and improving selection of wine, rum, ouzo, vodka, gin, tequila and some liqueurs, and bottles its own cognac, brandy and whisky.

All these are drinkable but not of international standard. In the light of these restrictions, most Zimbabweans greatly appreciate gifts of duty-free imported wines and liquor from visitors.

There is a reasonably wide range of the well-known soft drinks and Mazoe orange and lime cordials are especially recommended. For camping foods see What to Take, Chapter 6 (page 134).

Telephone system

With patience, most international calls can be dialled direct, although some exchanges are particularly difficult, e.g. Kariba. Local services are often disrupted during the rains. Public phones are widely available in the main centres.

Under Zimbabwe's relatively antiquated telephone system each exchange has its own dialling code. In this book these codes have been inserted in brackets before the main telephone number. Where codes include a dash, you should wait for a second dialling tone before continuing to dial the main number.

Arcturus	174	Makuti	163
Banket	*166	Marondera	179
Beatrice	165	Mashava	135
Beitbridge	186	Masvingo	139
Bindura	171	Mataga	151–7***
Binga	115	Matobo	183–8
Bulawayo	19	Mazowe	175
Centenary	157	Mberengwa	151–8*
Chakari	168–8	Mhangura	160
Chatsworth	130–8**	Mount Darwin	176*
Chegutu	153	Munyati	155–7

Zimbabwe

Chimanimani	126	Murambinda	121
Chinhoyi	167	Murewa	178
Chipangoyi	124	Mutare	120*
Chipinge	127	Mutoko	172*
Chiredzi	131	Mutoroshanga	166–8*
Chirundu	163–7	Mvuma	132*
Chitungwiza	170	Mvurwi	177
Chivu	156	Mwenezi	114–7***
Concession	175–6	Ngundu	136***
Darwendale	169*	Nkayi	155–8***
Dete	118	Norton	162
Esigodini	188	Nyamandhlovu	187
Figtree	183	Nyanga	129–8
Filabusi	117	Nyazura	125–83*
Glendale	175–8	Nyika	138*
Gokwe	159	Odzi	120–4*
Guruve	158*	Penhalonga	120–5
Gutu	130*	Plumtree	180
Gwanda	184	Raffingora	166–7*
Gweru	154	Rusape	125
Harare	14	Rutenga	114*
Hauna	128***	Ruwa	173
Headlands	125–8*	Sanyati	168–7
Hwange	181	Selous	162–8
Jerera	134*	Shamva	172–8*
Jotsholo	189	Shangani	150
Juliasdale	129	Shurugwi	152
Kadoma	168	Trelawney	169–8*
Kariba	161	Triangle	133
Karoi	164	Turk Mine	185
Kezi	182	Victoria Falls	113
Kwekwe	155	Wedza	122*
Lalapanzi	154–83	West Nocholson	116
Lupane	189–8**	Zvishavane	151
Macheke	179–8		

*   Exchanges to be converted from manual to automatic in future.
**   Manual exchanges.
*** Exchanges to be opened in the future.

Bear in mind that since this book was written, numbers may have changed. If you have problems in trying to get through, try dialling the international operator on 96 or Directory Enquiries on 92.

Postal service

Slow but generally reliable. Don't post anything valuable without registering it first. Hours of business of post offices: Monday to Friday 08:30 to 16:00. The main post office in Harare, which is at the corner of Inez Terrace and George Silundika Avenue, opens at 08:00. Saturday business hours are 08:00 to 11:30.

Tipping

A tip of 10 per cent is usually acceptable, except when a service charge is already added to the bill.

Travel agencies and airlines

For a list of airlines flying to and within Zimbabwe see Chapter 4, How to get there (page 93).

For a list of travel agencies, safari operators and touring organisations, see Chapter 5, Travelling inside Zimbabwe (page 79).

Gambling

Kariba, Juliasdale, Victoria Falls and Vumba all have casinos. In Kariba the casino is at Caribbea Bay Resort, while in Victoria Falls there are two, one at Makasa Sun Hotel and the other at the Elephant Hills Hotel. In the Eastern Highlands area there is one at the Montclair Casino Hotel in Juliasdale, and another is due to be opened at Leopard Rock Hotel in the Vumba Mountains near Mutare.

Television, radio and press

Television is offered on two channels. A portion of the material is locally produced while the bulk is from the United Kingdom and the USA. Programmes are broadcast in colour although most TV sets are in black and white.

The Zimbabwe Broadcasting Corporation (ZBC) offers four stations: Radio 1 – English talk and classical music; Radio 2 – Shona and Ndebele; Radio 3 – British and American pop music; Radio 4 – educational and cultural.

BBC World Service transmission times in GMT are as follows:

05:00 – 07:30 : 12.095
09:00 – 15:15 : 21.71 Mhz and 17.79 Mhz
20:00 – 22:45 : 6.195

Remember to add two hours to GMT for local time.

There are two national daily newspapers, *The Herald* (published in Harare) which sells about 140 000 copies, and *The Chronicle* (published in Bulawayo) which sells about 60 000 copies. There are two Sunday papers, the *Sunday Mail* (Harare 140 000 copies) and *The Sunday News* (Bulawayo). The weekly *Financial Gazette* (21 000 copies), which gives a broader spread of international news, is published on Friday. Note that newspapers are in short supply on street corners, in hotels and bookshops. If you intend to read the paper, make sure you get it early in the morning or ask your hotel to reserve a copy for you the next day. If you like reading international magazines such as *Time* and *Newsweek*, be prepared to go without as they are difficult to find. Bring your own periodicals if your holiday is not going to be too long as only a very small range of English-language magazines and periodicals are available in bookshops and on street corners in the larger towns.

Electricity

220–240 AC voltage throughout Zimbabwe. Both round and square pin plugs are used so bring an adaptor that can take both types.

Photography

Bring your own film to be on the safe side but it is often obtainable in the larger centres. There are a few 24-hour processing laboratories in Harare, Bulawayo and Victoria Falls which produce reasonable quality at reasonable prices. Don't leave your camera or films lying in the heat as they may be damaged. Always try to keep films cool – the fridge is the best place for them.

You may not find batteries for your camera or video camera so either replace them before you leave home or bring spares with you. Always pay others the courtesy of asking for permission before taking photographs of people and/or their possessions and houses. Expect to be asked for a small payment or to send copies of the photograph by mail when you return home.

Do not photograph anything strategic such as bridges, prisons, military and police buildings and staff, airports and refugee camps.

The best time of day to take photographs in Zimbabwe is either in the early morning or late afternoon. The sunlight is so bright, especially towards midday, that unsightly shadows are cast over subjects' faces.

A telephoto lens (minimum 200 mm) will give you best results in photographing game, and the panoramic vistas are best taken with a wide-angle lens. Because of the dusty conditions during the dry season it is essential to bring good lens cleaning equipment as well as an ultra violet filter.

Sport and entertainment

See Chapter 3.

Useful addresses

Conservation, wildlife

The Wildlife Society of Zimbabwe, P. O Box 3497 Harare. Headquarters, Mukuvisi woodlands, Glenara Avenue South, Hillside, Harare, Tel (14) 73–1596.

The Zambezi Society, P. O. Box UA334 Union Avenue, Harare. The society promotes the conservation of the Zambezi River and the land on its banks.

Tourist information

The Zimbabwe Tourist Development Corporation, Tourism House, Fourth Street/Stanley Avenue, P. O. Box 8052 Causeway, Harare, Tel (14) 7–9366.

North America

Zimbabwe Tourist Office, Rockefeller Centre, Suite 1905, 1270 Avenue of the Americas, New York, New York 10020, United States of America, Tel 1–(212)3076565/6568.

South Africa

Zimbabwe Tourist Office, Upper Shopping Level, Carlton Centre, Commissioner Street, P. O. Box 9398, Johannesburg 2000, Republic of South Africa, Tel (2711) 331-3137.

Europe

Zimbabwe Tourist Office, Steinweg 9, D-6000 Frankfurt am Main 1, Frankfurt, Germany, Tel (49-69)-294042/3.

United Kingdom, Ireland and Scandinavia

Zimbabwe Tourist Office, Zimbabwe High Commission, 429 Strand, London WC2R 05A, Tel 07-836-7755.

Elsewhere

Try your nearest Zimbabwe embassy or high commission.

Service organisations

Round Table, P. O. Box 2969 Harare, Tel (14) 72-20764.
Rotary, Stewart House, Cental Avenue, Harare, P. O. Box 2330, Harare, Tel (14) 70-2095.
Lions, P. O. Box 8396, Harare, Tel (14) 73-5811.

Diplomatic representatives in Zimbabwe

If you wish to travel on to any other country in Africa, it is best to obtain your entry visa, if one is required, in your home country to avoid any delays.

Algeria	8 Pascoe Avenue, Belgravia, Harare. Tel (14) 72-6619/72-6682
Angola	Doncaster House, Speke Avenue, Harare, Tel (14) 79-0675/79-0070
Argentina	10th Floor Club Chambers, Baker Avenue, Harare, Tel (14) 73-0075/6
Australia	4th Floor Karigamombe Centre, Samora Machel Avenue, Harare, Tel (14) 79 4591/70-1456
Austria	Trade Commission, 6th floor Globe House, 51 Jason Moyo Avenue, P. O. Box 1850, Harare, Tel (14) 70-4600

Miscellaneous information

Bangladesh	8 Birchenough Road, Old Alexandra Park, Harare, Tel (14) 72–7004
Belgium	8th Floor NCR House, Samora Machel Avenue, Harare, Tel (14) 79–3306/7
Botswana	22 Philips Avenue, Belgravia, Harare, Tel (14) 72–9551/3
Brazil	9th Floor Old Mutual Centre, 3rd Street/Stanley Avenue, Harare, Tel (14) 73–0775
Bulgaria	15 Maasdorp Avenue, Alexandra Park, Harare, Tel (14) 73–0509
Canada	45 Baines Avenue, Moffat St, Harare, Tel (14) 73–3881
China	30 Baines Avenue, Harare, Tel (14) 72–4572
Cuba	5 Philips Avenue, Belgravia, Harare, Tel (14) 72–0256/7
Czechoslovakia	104 Vanguard House, Stanley Avenue/4th Street, Harare, Tel (14) 70–0636
Denmark	1st Floor UDC Centre, 59 Union Avenue, Harare, Tel (14) 73–2541/4
Egypt	7 Aberdeen Road, Avondale, Harare, Tel (14) 30–3445/30–3497
Ethiopia	14 Lanark Road, Belgravia, Harare, Tel (14) 72–5822
Finland	3rd Floor, Karigamombe Centre, Samora Machel Avenue, Harare, Tel (14) 70–7344/70–0943
France	Ranelagh Road, off Orange Grove Drive Highlands, Harare, Tel (14) 4–8096/8
Germany	2 Ceres Road, Avondale, Harare, Tel (14) 73–1955
Ghana	11 Downie Avenue, Belgravia, Harare, Tel (14) 73–8652
Greece	8 Deary Road, Belgravia, Harare, Tel (14) 72–3747
Hungary	29 Lanark Road, Belgravia, Harare, Tel (14) 72–3747
India	12 Natal Road, Belgravia, Harare, Tel (14) 79–5955
Indonesia	26 Wavell Road, Highlands, Harare, Tel (14) 4–6809/73–2561

178 Zimbabwe

Iran	8 Allan Wilson Avenue, Belgravia, Harare, Tel (14) 72-7348
Iraq	21 Lawson Avenue, Milton Park, Harare, Tel (14) 72-5727
Italy	7 Bartholomew Close, Off Dulwich Road, Greendale, Harare, Tel (14) 4-7279/4-8199
Japan	Level 5 Pegasus House, 52 Samora Machel Avenue, Harare, Tel (14) 72-7500/7-2769
Kenya	95 Park Lane, Harare, Tel (14) 79-2901
Korea (North)	102 Josiah Chinamano Avenue, Harare, Tel (14) 72-4052/72-4067
Libya	124-126 Harare Street, Harare, Tel (14) 72-8381/3
Malawi	42-44 Harare Street, Harare, Tel (14) 70-5611
Mozambique	152 Rhodes Avenue, Harare, Tel (14) 79-0837
Netherlands	47 Enterprise Road, Highlands, Harare, Tel (14) 73-1428
New Zealand	Batanai Gardens, Jason Moyo Avenue, Harare, Tel (14) 72-8681/6
Nicaragua	9 Downie Avenue, Belgravia, Harare, Tel (14) 70-1280
Nigeria	36 Samora Machel Avenue, Harare, Tel (14) 79-0785
Norway	92 Josiah Chinamaro Avenue, Harare, Tel (14) 79-2419
Pakistan	11 Van Praagh Avenue, Milton Park, Harare, Tel (14) 72-0293
Peru	Eighth Floor, Zimnat House, 3rd Street/Baker Avenue, Harare, Tel (14) 73-6751
Poland	16 Cork Road, Belgravia, Harare, Tel (14) 73-2159
Portugal	10 Samora Machel Avenue, Harare, Tel (14) 72-5107
Romania	105 Eden Rock Building, 4th Street, Harare, Tel (14) 70-0853/72-5493
South Africa	Temple Bar House, 39 Baker Street, Harare, Tel (14) 70-7901

Spain	16 Philips Avenue, Belgravia, Harare, Tel (14) 73-8681/2
Sudan	4 Pascoe Avenue, Belgravia, Harare, Tel (14) 72-5240
Sweden	7th Floor, Pegasus House, 52 Samora Machel Avenue, Harare, Tel (14) 79-0651
Switzerland	9 Lanark Road, Belgravia, Harare, Tel (14) 70-3997
Tanzania	Ujamaa House, Blakiston/Baines avenues, Harare, Tel (14) 72-4173
Togo	13 Bath Road, Belgravia, Harare, Tel (14) 73-8695
Tunisia	5 Ashton Road, Alexandra Park, Harare, Tel (14) 79-1570
United Kingdom	6th Floor Stanley House, Stanley Avenue/1st Street, Harare, Tel (14) 79-3781
United States	172 Herbert Chitepo Avenue, Harare, Tel (14) 79-4521
USSR (now CIS)	70 Fife Avenue, Belgravia, Harare, Tel (14) 72-0358
Vietnam	14 Carlisle Drive, Alexandra Park, Harare, Tel (14) 70-1118
Yugoslavia	1 Lanark Road, Belgravia, Harare, Tel (14) 73-8668
Zaire	5 Pevensey Road, off Enterprise Road (some 8 km from the centre), Tel (14) 73-0893
Zambia	6th Floor Zambia House, Union Avenue, (near Julius Nyerere Street), Harare, Tel (14) 79-0851

Zimbabwean diplomatic representation abroad

Algeria	5 Chemin des Bicillars, Mausareah, Algiers
Belgium	21-22 Avenue des Arts, B-1040 Brussels
Botswana	IGI Building, 1st Floor, P. O. Box 1232, Gaborone
Canada	112 Kent St, Place de Ville, Suite 915, Tower 'B' Ottawa, Ontario K1p 5PT.
China	No. 62, Entrance 2, Office building for Diplomatic Personnel, San-Li-Tun, Peking
Ethiopia	P. O. Box 5624, Addis Ababa
Germany	Victoriastrasse 28, 5300, Bonn 2, Bonn

France	5 Rue de Tilsitt, Paris, 75008
Japan	11–23 Minami Azabu, 3 Chome Mulatoku, Tokyo, 106
Kenya	6th Floor, ICDC Building, P. O. Box 30806, Nairobi
Malawi	Zimbabwe High Commission, New Town, Lilongwe, P. O. Box 30187, Lilongwe 3
Mozambique	P. O. Box 743, Maputo
Nigeria	6 Kasumu Ekemonde St, Victoria Island, Lagos
Romania	6 Visaron Street, P. O. Box 22–164, Bucharest
Sweden	Oxtoget 5, 10390, Stockholm
Switzerland	250 Rue de Lausanne, Chemin du Rivage, 1292 Chambesy, Geneva.
Tanzania	Plot 439, Maliki Road, Upanda West, Dar es Salaam
United Kingdom	429 The Strand, London WC2
USA	2851 McGill Terrace, NW, Washington DC 20008
Yugoslavia	Jogoslavaja Hotel, Room 306, Belgrade
Zambia	4th Floor, Ulendo House, Cairo Road, Lusaka

INDEX

Accidents 111
Accommodation 136, 139, 151, 155, 157
Bulawayo 136
Chimanimani National Park 138, 155
Chizarira National Park 156
Gonarezhou National Park 139, 140, 156
Great Zimbabwe 140
Harare 141
Hwange National Park 140, 144, 150, 156
Lake Chivero 157
Lake Kariba 146, 147
Lake Mutirikwi 140, 151, 158
Mana Pools National Park 149, 158
Mare Dam 159
Matobo National Park 158
Matusadona National Park 159
Nyanga National Park 145, 151, 159
Rhodes Dam 159
Udu Dam 159
Victoria Falls 152
Zambezi National Park 159
AIDS 131
Air links 93
Air transport 123
  charter companies 124
  charter flights 123
  Flame Lily Holidays 124
Airport tax 99
Angling 75
  International Tigerfishing Contest 40, 75
  licences and permits 75
  trout fishing 76
  tackle 75
Art Gallery, Bulawayo 22
Automobile Association 111

Balloon safaris 77
Banks 165
Bilharzia 129
Binga 54
Birdwatching 68, 69
  Lake Chivero 69

Larvon Bird Gardens 69
Mukuvisi woodlands 69
Zambezi Valley 70
Boat transport 125
  charter companies 125
  Lake Kariba 125
Boating 66
  Lake Chivero 66
  Lake Kariba 66
  Lake Mutirikwi 66
Border posts 94
Botanical reserves 127
Bridal Veil Falls 27
Bulawayo 18, 24, 70, 119
  access by air 21
  access by road 21
  access by train 21
  accommodation 136
  Art Gallery 22
  Centenary Park 22
  Central Park 23
  Chipangali Wildlife Trust 24
  crafts 72
  Cyrene Mission 24
  Dhlodhlo/Danangombe ruins 23
  Jairos Jiri shop 22
  Khame ruins 23
  map 19
  Mzilikazi art and craft centre 22
  Naletale ruins 23
  National Natural History Museum 21
  Railway Museum 22
  restaurants 163
  tourist information 20
  Tshabalala Sanctuary 24
  souvenirs 72
Bumi Hills 54
Bus transport 105
Bush etiquette 25
Business hours 166

Camping gear 135
Canoeing safaris 66 67
  Lake Kariba 67
  Zambezi River 66

Centenary Park, Bulawayo 22
Central Park, Bulawayo 23
Chapungu Kraal 16
Chimanimani National Park 25, 62, 116
  access 27
  accommodation 138, 155
  hiking 62
  map 26
  walking 62
Chinhoyi Caves 122
Chipangali animal orphanage 119
Chipangali Wildlife Trust 24
Chizarira National Park 28, 29
  access 29
  accommodation 156
  wilderness trails 65
Climate 3, 126
Clothing 133
Connemara lakeland 63
Crafts 70
Cricket 92
Currency regulations 98
Customs 168
  duty 97
Cycling 106
Cyrene Mission 24

Dentists 132
Dhlodhlo/Danangombe ruins 23, 123
Diana's Vow rock paintings 113
Diplomatic representatives 176
Domboshawa rock paintings 17
Dress 99
Driving etiquette 107
Driving hazards 111
Driving licences 100

Eastern Highlands 62
  birdwatching 69
Economy 4
Eland Sanctuary 27
Electricity 174
Epworth balancing rocks 17
Ewanrigg Botanical Gardens 17

Facilities 165
Firearms 97
First-aid kit 132
Fishing 89
  see also angling
Food and drink 134, 170, 173
Fothergill Island 54
Fuel 104

Gambling 89, 173, 175
Geography 3
Golf 90
Gonarezhou National Park 30
  access 30
  accommodation 139, 140, 156
Government 8
  ministries and departments 167
Great Zimbabwe 5, 47, 48, 117, 151
  access 48
  accommodation 140
Greenwood Park 15

Harare 9, 15
  access by air 12
  access by car 13
  access by train 12
  accommodation 141
  birdwatching 69
  Chapungu Kraal 16
  crafts 71
  Domboshawa rock paintings 17
  Epworth balancing rocks 17
  Ewanrigg Botanical gardens 17
  Gardens 14
  Greenwood Park 15
  Heroes' Acre 16
  history 9
  Lake Chivero 17
  Larvon Bird Gardens 18
  Lion and cheetah park 18
  Macgregor Geological Museum 15
  map 10
  Mbare market 11, 13
  Mukuvisi woodlands 16
  National archives 13
  National Botanical Gardens 15
  National gallery 14
  National Handicraft Centre 15
  National museum 14
  restaurants 160
  snake park 18
  souvenirs 71
  tourist information 12
Health certificates 99
Health precautions 128
Heroes' Acre 16
Hiking 62
  Chimanimani National Park 62
  Eastern Highlands 62
  Nyanga National Park 62

Hippo Pool   60
History   5
Hitchhiking   105
Holidays   170
Honde Valley   41, 115
Horse racing   92
Horseback safaris   78
Hunting safaris   78
Hwange National Park   31, 120
  access   33
  accommodation   140, 144, 156
  birdwatching   69
  map   32
  wilderness trails   65

Imire Game Park   113
Immigration requirements   96
Inoculations   132
International Tigerfishing Contest   40, 75

Jairos Jiri, Bulawayo   22
Journalists, accreditation   98

Kandahar Island   60
Kariba   121, 127
  see also Lake Kariba
Khame ruins   5, 23, 123

Lake Chivero National Park   34
  access   34
  accommodation   157
  birdwatching   69
Lake Kariba   49, 55
  access   52
  accommodation   146, 147
  air charter   55
  boat charter   55
  boat transport   125
  boating/yachting   66
  canoeing safaris   67
  car hire   55
  crafts   74
  cruises   53
  hotels   56
  map   50
  safaris and tours   55
  souvenirs   74
Lake Mutirikwi   117, 140, 151, 158
Language   168
Larvon Bird Gardens   18, 69
Lion and cheetah park, Harare   18

Macgregor Geological Museum   15

Makuti   122
Malaria   128
Maleme Dam   38
Mana Pools National Park   35, 127
  access   35
  accommodation   149, 158
  map   36
  wilderness trails   65
Maps   62, 107
Mare Dam   159
Matetsi Safari Region   65
Matobo National Park   37, 119
  access   37
  accommodation   158
  walking   65
Matusadona National Park   38
  access   40
  accommodation   159
  map   39
  walking safaris   64
Mbare market, Harare   11, 13
Mlibizi   54
Motor insurance   99
Motor licences   99
Motor vehicles   99
Mount Nyangani   42, 62
Mountain Club of Zimbabwe   28, 62
Mtarazi Falls   41, 114
Mtarazi National Park   41
  access   41
Mukuvisi woodlands   16, 69
  walking safaris   65
Mzilikazi art and craft centre, Bulawayo   22

Naletale ruins   23, 123
Name changes   107
National archives, Harare   13
National Botanical Gardens   15
National flag   8
National gallery, Harare   14
National Handicraft Centre   15
National museum, Harare   14
National Natural History Museum, Bulawayo   21
National parks   24, 127
  access   35
  accommodation   155
  booking   155
  bush etiquette   25
  Chimanimani   25

Index 183

184 Zimbabwe

Chizarira 28
Gonarezhou 30
Hwange 31
information 24
Lake Chivero 34
Mana Pools 35
Matobo 37
Matusadona 38
Mtarazi 41
Nyanga 42
Victoria Falls 44
walking safaris 64
wilderness trails 65
Zambezi 46
Newspapers 174
Nyanga National Park 42, 62, 114
  access 42
  accommodation 145, 151, 159
  hiking 62
  map 43
  walking 62
Nyanga region
  crafts 73
  souvenirs 73
Nyangombe Falls 63

Overland operators 96
Ox-wagon safaris 77

Pets 99
Photographic safaris 78
Photography 135, 174
Population 7
Postal service 173, 175
Public holidays 170
Pungwe Drift 64
Pungwe Falls 41, 64, 115
Pungwe Gorge 41, 115

Radio 174
Rail safaris 78
Rail transport 124
Railway Museum, Bulawayo 22
Restaurants 160
Rhodes Dam 159
Road links 94
Road transport 101
Routes see standard routes
Rugby 92
Ruins 5, 23
  Dhlodhlo/Danangombe 23, 123
  Great Zimbabwe 5, 47
  Khame 5, 23, 123

Naletale 23, 123
Ziwa 42

Safari operators 79
Safaris 76, 78
  balloon 77
  horseback 78
  hunting 78
  ox-wagon 77
  photographic 78
  rail 78
  sailing 77
Safety precautions 133
Sailing safaris 77
Sanyati Gorge 54
Scorpions 131
Seasons 126
Security 165
Shoes 134
Shopping 166
Snake park, Harare 18
Snakes 130
Soccer 92
Souvenirs 70
Speed limits 107
Spiders 131
Sporting equipment 134
Spurwing Island 53
Squash 89
Standard routes 112
  Bulawayo to Harare 123
  Bulawayo to Victoria Falls 119
  Chimanimani to Masvingo 116
  Harare to Nyanga 112
  Kariba to Harare 121
  Masvingo to Bulawayo 118
  Mutare to Chimanimani 115
  Nyanga to Mutare 114
  Victoria Falls to Kariba 121
Sunburn 131
Swimming 89

Taxis 107
Telephone system 171, 173
Television 174
Tennis 89
Tickbite fever 130
Tipping 173
Toghwe Wilderness area 65
Tourist information
  Bulawayo 20
  Harare 12

Travel agencies see Wildlife Producers Co-op
Trout fishing   76
Troutbeck   114, 152
Tshabalala Sanctuary   24

Udu Dam   159
Useful addresses   175
Useful words and phrases   169

Vegetation   4
Vehicle hire   102
Vehicle security   101
Vehicle spares   100
Victoria Falls National Park   44
   access   44
Victoria Falls   57, 120, 127
   access   59
   accommodation   152
   crafts   73
   map   45
   souvenirs   73
   walking safaris   65
Visas   96

Walking   62
   Chimanimani National Park   62
   Eastern Highlands   62
   Matobo National Park   65

Nyanga National Park   62
Walking safaris   64
   Matusadona National Park   64
   Mukuvisi woodlands   65
   Victoria Falls   65
Watersport   66
White rhino shelter   38
White water rafting   67
Wilderness trails   65
   Chizarira National Park   65
   Hwange National Park   65
   Mana Pools National Park   65
Wildlife Producers Co-operative   79
World's View   38, 63

Yachting   66
   Lake Chivero   66
   Lake Kariba   66
   Lake Mutirikwi   66

Zambezi National Park   46
   access   46
   accommodation   159
Zambezi River
   canoeing safaris   66
   white water rafting   67
Zambezi Valley
   birdwatching   70
Zimbabwe ruins see Great Zimbabwe
Ziwa ruins   42

ORIENTATION MAP
ZIMBABWE IN SOUTHERN AFRICA

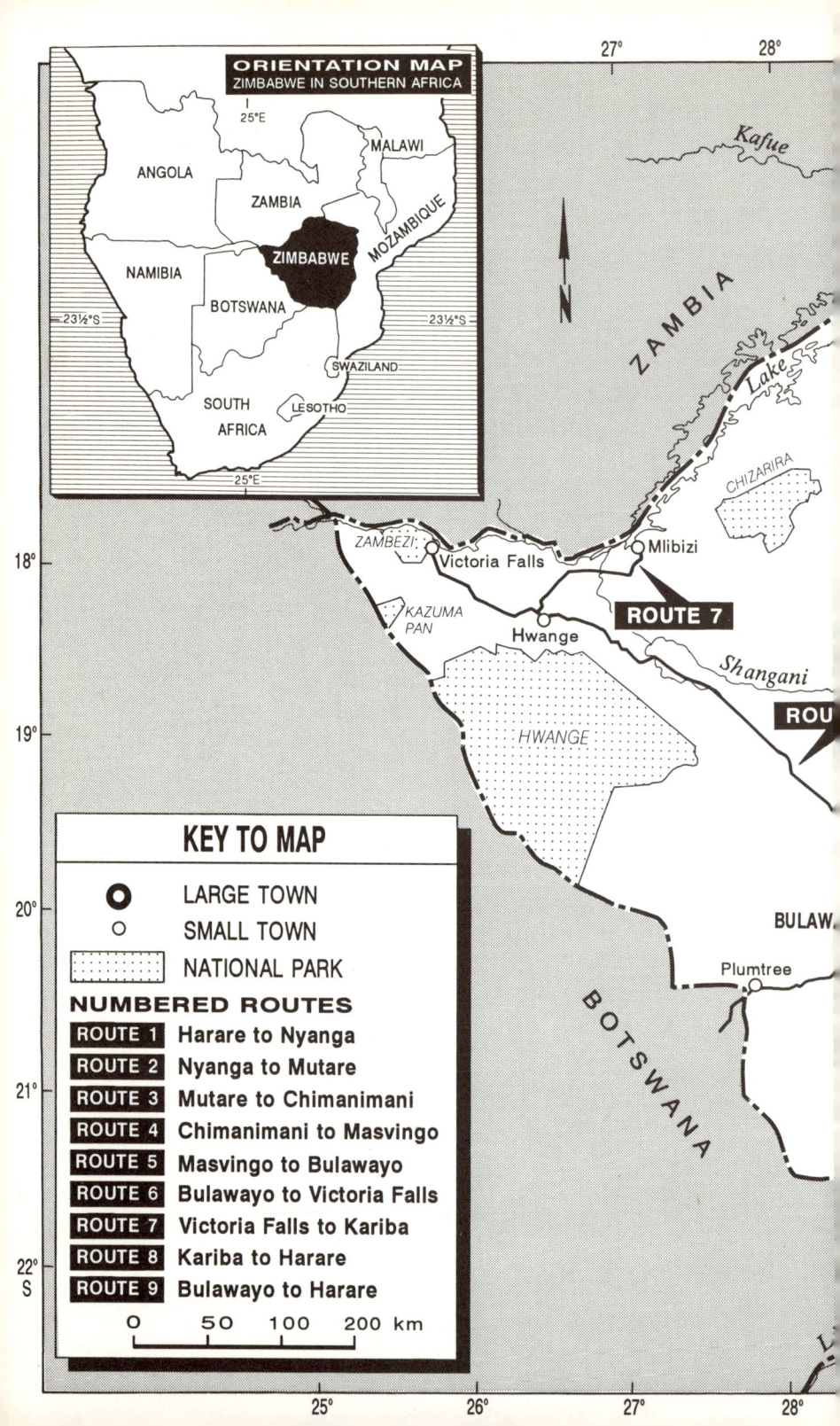

ANGOLA
MALAWI
ZAMBIA
MOZAMBIQUE
ZIMBABWE
NAMIBIA
BOTSWANA
SWAZILAND
SOUTH AFRICA
LESOTHO

Kafue
ZAMBIA
Lake
CHIZARIRA
ZAMBEZI
Victoria Falls
Mlibizi
KAZUMA PAN
Hwange
ROUTE 7
Shangani
HWANGE
ROU
BULAW
Plumtree
BOTSWANA

KEY TO MAP

◎ LARGE TOWN
○ SMALL TOWN
▫ NATIONAL PARK

NUMBERED ROUTES

ROUTE 1	Harare to Nyanga
ROUTE 2	Nyanga to Mutare
ROUTE 3	Mutare to Chimanimani
ROUTE 4	Chimanimani to Masvingo
ROUTE 5	Masvingo to Bulawayo
ROUTE 6	Bulawayo to Victoria Falls
ROUTE 7	Victoria Falls to Kariba
ROUTE 8	Kariba to Harare
ROUTE 9	Bulawayo to Harare

0 50 100 200 km